Evergreen

Living with Plants

gestalten

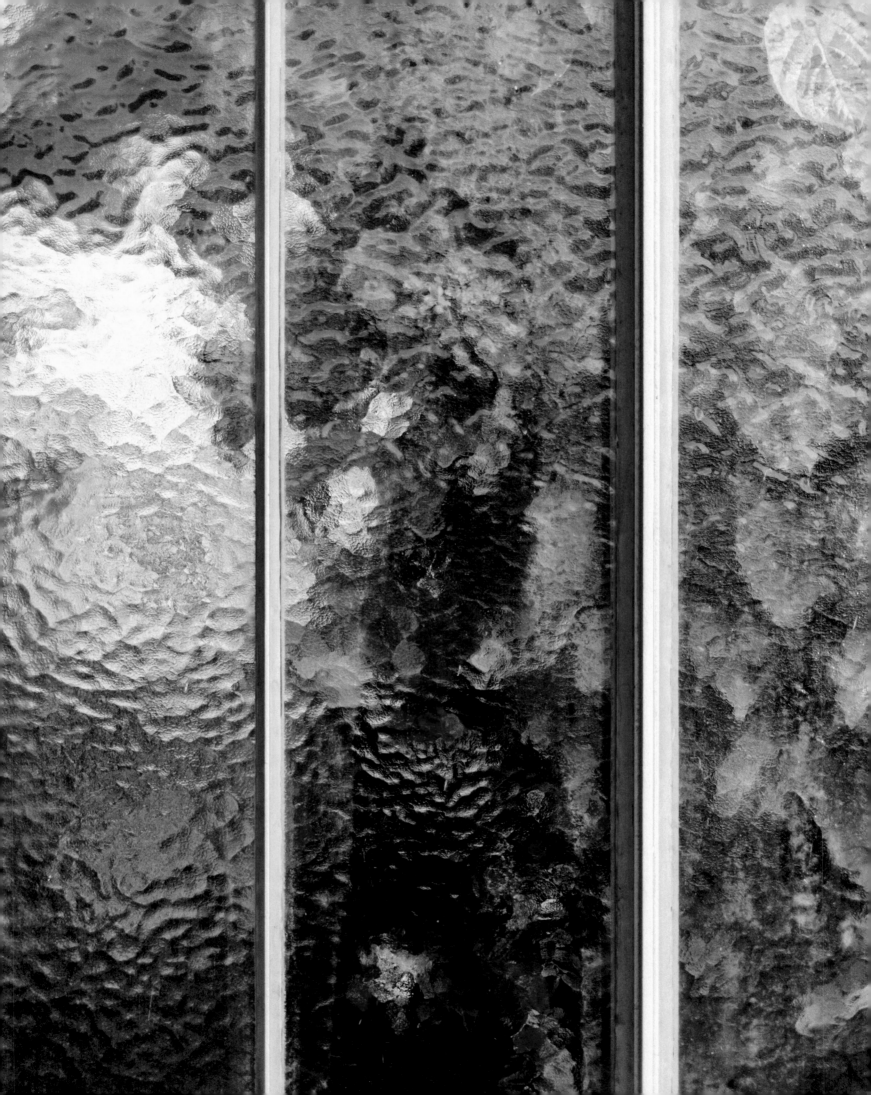

Swooning Over Nature

The education of a gardener begins with aesthetics. More than ever though, gardening has become important as not only an activity or hobby, but as an attitude, punctuated by sustainable and wholesome living. Swooning a new generation of gardeners, modern homes are transforming into green habitats and city dwellers' points of refuge, bubbling with character and warmth. Demanding intimacy, attention, and care, plants inspire us to become more intuitive dwellers; reflecting owners' capabilities of cohabitation and engagement with the natural world. Indeed, setting up the right conditions for plants to breath and develop permits that a home's inhabitants, and its guests, too, feel welcome and at ease.

Beyond the fashionable factor, modern gardens are maximizing horticultural potential. From floral workshops to cactus fares and farmers' markets almost inflicting the green thumb upon us, to whole residential projects designed around the essential component of bamboo, to cafés mimicking overgrown orchards, and restaurants flaunting their locally-sourced initiatives. Because the modern world demands a detachment from our natural environment, our relationship with nature is an ever-more comforting, tactile, and important one.

Gardens, whether in the form of a petite collection of herbs, geraniums tucked inside a balcony container, or a sprawling six-acre oasis, all have some kind of stylistic vision behind them. They can be subtle and instinctive, they can be contrasting and confusing, and they can be full-on self-realizations. In our indoor gardens, we often seek colors and textures, and often we are rewarded with a new relationship to the space that both we and our plants inhabit. On our balconies and terraces, we look for a revered room to call our own. In our backyards, the greatest joy comes from plucking the first fruit from a nurtured tree. For the professional gardener, the highest reward comes with a garden's graceful progression through the seasons. Perhaps what makes gardening so satisfying is its continuity, because, unlike other activities, a gardener's work is never really complete. Florists, gardeners, and landscape architects around the world share a capability in transforming an empty lot into something better; envisioning something more, and infusing it with new life. At the same time, they are inspiring a new breed of plant-focused stores, magazines, and digital channels. Gardening, as a reminder of evanescence and imperfection, defines the utmost luxury of humility.

In indoor environments, plants benefit health and wellbeing by filtering the air of toxins and replenishing oxygen levels. And they invite optimism, too. The deep green tint of ivy leaves, curling down from a top shelf to cast shadows at just the right time of day, or the scent of spring's first tulips, bunched up in a tabletop vase, make for simple pleasures. During the winter, a fern can illuminate a darkened corner; a collection of homegrown herbs can color in our kitchen, and our homemade dishes, too. Throughout this book, readers can get a grasp on the basics of making and maintaining a patch of green: an empty kitchen windowsill; an unused balcony; a rejected backyard. Some properties collected in these pages are very much built to the beat of nature's drum; others more subtly incorporate the garden. Some are family homes; others are artist's studios. While gardens speak to aesthetics, they are also about discovery, in that they not only adorn a place, but act as a tie between us and the places we inhabit.

Turning a leaf towards sustainable living, we step into the backyards, rooftops, and empty lots that are being reimagined as ecological playing ground; the grounds of both harvested produce and the bringing-together of cultural communities. In the great outdoors, we tour public gardens, botanical gardens, wide-open cactus parks, and ecological farms, and introduce the people behind them. Gardens might be products of their environment, defined by temperature, materials, and means, but as such they nurture our craving for locality, for being as close as possible to the root of things. Especially in urban environments, the "excavation" of nature and the revalorizing of open space into sustainable landscapes opens new streams of interaction between us and the land.

For beginner gardeners, but for seasoned gardeners, too, the soundest advice is to garden as you can. To get your bearings, to get to know your plants, and to understand their likes and dislikes through smell and touch. As the famed twentieth century landscape gardener Russell Page wrote in his book The Education of a Gardener, the old expression of having a "green thumb" or "green fingers" describes "the art of communicating the subtle energies of love to prosper a living plant." It is with time that we come to recognize a plant's cultural needs, through idiosyncrasies of color, texture, and habit, he continues. Indeed, fears of overwatering and under-nurturing speak true to all stories of plants and people at the start of their relationship. In a combination of guidance and inspiration, our sustaining of a green habitat naturally begins to take its course, and with that, a greener lifestyle. The great outdoors is literally at your fingertips. ———•

Getting Your Bearings

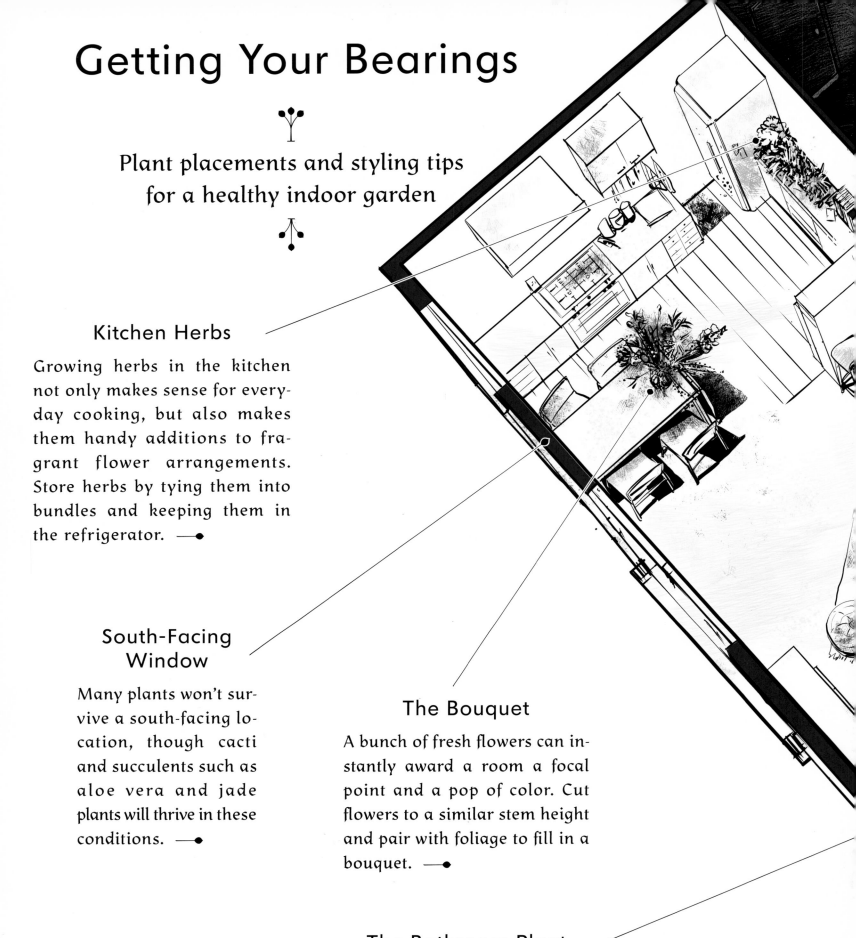

Plant placements and styling tips
for a healthy indoor garden

Kitchen Herbs

Growing herbs in the kitchen not only makes sense for everyday cooking, but also makes them handy additions to fragrant flower arrangements. Store herbs by tying them into bundles and keeping them in the refrigerator. —•

South-Facing Window

Many plants won't survive a south-facing location, though cacti and succulents such as aloe vera and jade plants will thrive in these conditions. —•

The Bouquet

A bunch of fresh flowers can instantly award a room a focal point and a pop of color. Cut flowers to a similar stem height and pair with foliage to fill in a bouquet. —•

The Bathroom Plant

Tropical plants will thrive in rooms where there is plenty of moisture. Varieties include bamboo, aloe vera, snake plants, and orchids. —•

Dark Corners

Houseplants that can grow in darker places are the hardiest of the lot, including the Boston fern and cast iron plant. ⟶•

Tools of the Trade

Versatility and precision are vital qualities for indoor tools, features that can save on both space and time

Handy Helpers

These two common garden tools are among the best to keep flowerbeds in top shape. Both the trowel and the hand fork can be used to turn soil, mix fertilizer, weed, and dig holes for small or medium sized plants. The tines of the fork are especially suited to breaking up hard, compacted soil. ➤

Magnifying Glass

Every living organism appreciates a bit of close attention every now and again. The magnifying glass, while it might seem like a strictly professional tool, is actually a useful device that even amateur gardeners can utilize. After a little research, growers can easily spot early signs of disease and pest infestations, and take the necessary actions to minimize damage. Hand lenses or loupes are a compact addition to any toolkit, one that could make a world of difference to a plant's life. ➤

Watering Can

Watering indoor plants can be a messy process. Without the right instrument, it is often difficult to gain direct access to the soil, a hindrance that can see water go places where it should not. Small, nimble units with thin spouts are an easy solution to this problem, providing the indoor gardener with a tidy method of nurturing their plants.

Pots and Terrariums

In areas where space is low, or natural ground scarce, pots offer a functional and fluid solution to planting needs. Even inside the home or office, they can be arranged in neat clusters, or bigger statement plants can stand on their own. Terracotta and brass pots are timeless vessels that, when chosen correctly, can help mediate a plant's vitality onto a room. The same goes for macramé hanging pots, which are particularly flexible in terms of space. For tabletops and small nooks, a succulent-based terrarium delivers an animated focal point in a compact package.

Vases

Regardless of how lush and captivating an indoor garden might be, flower-filled vases are always a surefire way to dress up a room. Glass, metal, and ceramic vases are among the most common types, and decorative bottles makes a sustainable alternative. To give flowers a little extra life, trim the stems before setting them in water, which should be changed every few days. Another tip is mixing sugar and white vinegar with the water, creating a solution that delivers nutrients and protects against harmful bacteria. ——●

8

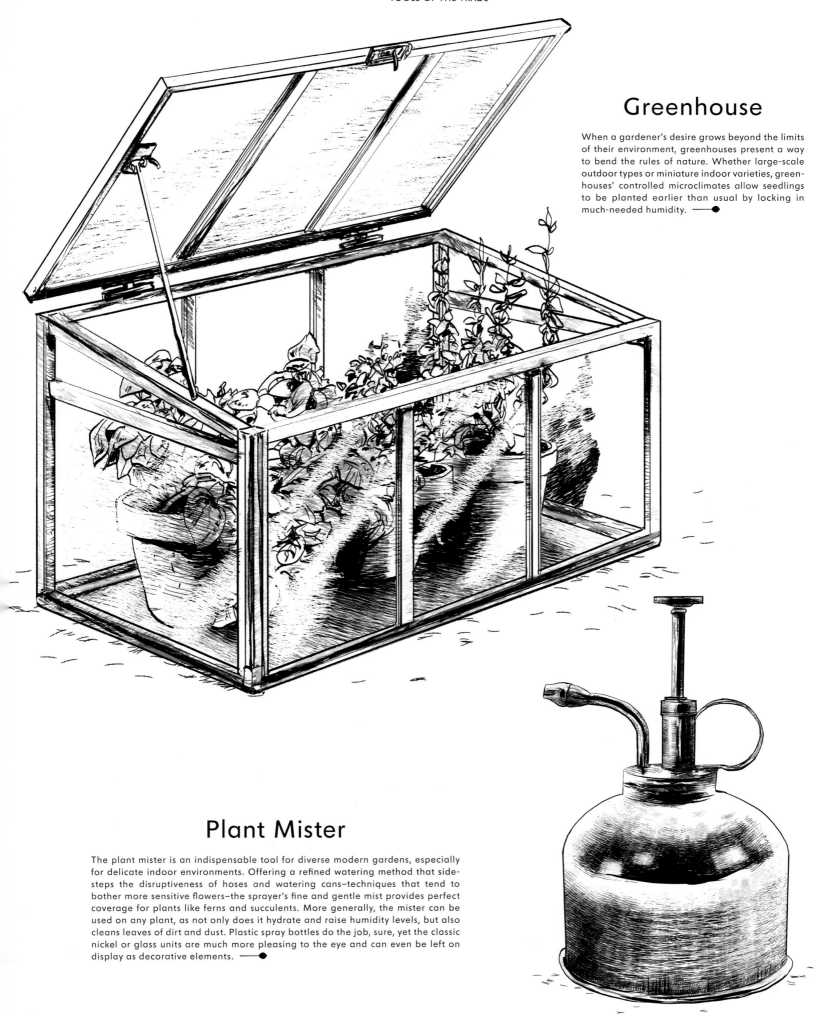

Greenhouse

When a gardener's desire grows beyond the limits of their environment, greenhouses present a way to bend the rules of nature. Whether large-scale outdoor types or miniature indoor varieties, greenhouses' controlled microclimates allow seedlings to be planted earlier than usual by locking in much-needed humidity. ——●

Plant Mister

The plant mister is an indispensable tool for diverse modern gardens, especially for delicate indoor environments. Offering a refined watering method that sidesteps the disruptiveness of hoses and watering cans—techniques that tend to bother more sensitive flowers—the sprayer's fine and gentle mist provides perfect coverage for plants like ferns and succulents. More generally, the mister can be used on any plant, as not only does it hydrate and raise humidity levels, but also cleans leaves of dirt and dust. Plastic spray bottles do the job, sure, yet the classic nickel or glass units are much more pleasing to the eye and can even be left on display as decorative elements. ——●

The Great Indoors

From miniature succulents to towering statement trees,
indoor plants that make an impact

Calathea

Calathea

Grown exclusively for its ornamental foliage, the calathea comes in many colors and with many names: zebra plant, peacock plant, or rattlesnake plant, based on its leaf markings. To avoid running the risk of losing the plant's color or burning its leaves, keep the calathea away from direct sunlight and look for a north-facing windowsill instead. Importantly, the calathea enjoys being watered very regularly, though without having to sit in a puddle. By the same token, its leaves will demand regular misting to stay healthy and bright. ———●

Origin Tropical South and Central America · Height 20–60 cm
Watering schedule Regular, small amounts of water, generally when the surface dries up

Asparagus Fern

Asparagus aethiopicus

Although called a fern, this houseplant belongs to the lily family, and comes covered in small leaflets that give it an airy look. This easy-to-grow lightweight looks great in hanging baskets or on tabletops, and is a safe–almost indestructible–choice for beginner gardeners. To keep it neat, trim back the stems in the spring, and repot the plant into a larger container after a growth spurt. Drooping leaves can be a sign of too much sunlight or of dry soil, though be wary of overwatering, as its thick roots are little water tanks. ———●

Origin South Africa · Height Stems can grow 30–90 cm long
Watering schedule Regularly and thoroughly, and more sparingly in the winter

Spider Plant

Chlorophytum comosum

Also known as the airplane plant, this plant's stringy pale green and yellow leaves will take all the sunlight they can get. Considered one of the most adaptable houseplants, spider plants are ideal for hanging baskets, which allow them to rotate for maximum light. Young spider plants produce small white flowers in the summer called spiderettes, which grow around the adult plant, and can easily be replanted in potting soil. ➝●

Origin **Africa** · Height **15 – 30 cm tall** · Watering schedule **Keep the soil mostly moist during spring, and fertilize twice a month**

11

String of Pearls

Senecio rowleyanus

A plant that grows well in bright light with good draining soil, the string of pearls plant makes a wonderful focal point to any indoor space, with its plump, round "leaves" spilling out of its container. As a succulent, the plant is in the easy-to-maintain category. Being very drought tolerant, the one problem you might have is regular pruning when the plant's arms become too long, although cut-off bits can easily be propagated in a pot of soil. ——●

Origin **Southwest Africa** · Height **30 – 90 cm cm in length**
Watering schedule **Thoroughly once a month**

Fiddle-Leaf Fig

Ficus lyrata

The fiddle-leaf fig is a modern-day statement plant. Native to the rainforests of Western Africa, it easily dresses up a room with its thin trunk and expressive, glossy green leaves. Although popular, fiddle-leafs are moody and difficult to maintain. Indirect sunlight and the right air temperature and humidity levels are essential, alongside regular cleaning of the leaves. Keep an eye on excess water before reaching for the watering can. ——●

Origin **West Africa** · Height **1 – 3 m indoors, and
up to 15 m in its natural habitat** · Watering schedule **Only when the
top layer of soil is dry, fluctuating with seasonal humidity**

Snake Plant/
Mother in Law's Tongue

Sansevieria

Recognizable by its long, upward-pointing leaves, this succulent's leaves are a strong green when healthy with a yellow tint around the edges. For forgetful gardeners, this houseplant will prove very forgiving, and even grows on a little neglect. A sunny windowsill is ideal, though its demands are low whether given full sun or a little shade. The ideal location is the bedroom: unlike other houseplants, the snake plant converts CO_2 into oxygen at night, a time during which other plants take it in. ———●

Origin West Africa · Height 15–30 cm tall · Watering schedule Every two weeks in summer, together with fertilizer, and very infrequently and no fertilizer during winter

English Ivy

Hedera helix

In NASA's survey of houseplants that filter harmful toxins and pollutants from the air, the English ivy was found to be one of the most effective. Adding texture to a tropical plant collection, ivy leaves require lots of indirect sunlight to maintain their color. Good drainage, regular washing of the leaves, and misting will keep this plant healthy. Monthly fertilization benefits the ivy's growth from spring through fall. ———●

Origin Europe · Height Depending on whether the surface is flat or for climbing, English ivy will grow as far as it is allowed to, usually between 5–20 cm Watering schedule Water weekly through spring and summer, and less during winter

Overcoming Gardener's Angst

From blanc canvas to green hideout:
Steps to organic success

Green It Like You Mean It

Consider the areas in your space that would benefit from some greening, and the different amounts of natural sunlight that these receive—whether direct or indirect—and look for plants that will thrive in these spots.

Think about the varying temperatures of your home. Different plants have different needs: placing a cool-temperature plant near a hot-air vent will make it weak and droopy, while placing a warm-temperature plant in a cooler spot will turn its leaves yellow.

Good to know: The grocery store might be closest, but it is worth locating shops that specialize in plants and garden utilities. Here you are most likely to find healthy plants and sound specialist advice. ——➤

Greening the Home from the Inside Out

Shopping for houseplants can be a nerve-wrecking task: the charm of creating an exotic home can easily wear thin in the haze of care labels, unknown specimens, and the wildly varying prices that you are faced with. Throw in variables such as local weather conditions, a cramped, possibly dimly lit space, and frequent trips away from home, and the thrill of dressing up your space with foliage can quickly pass. Gardener's angst is real. And it is fueled by our modern, everyday

activities that, by an ever-growing margin, demand a detachment from nature. Let's be clear: there is no such thing as a no-maintenance plant—but there are plants to match different environments and care calendars, and even some that thrive on a little neglect.

For beginner gardeners, it is important to get a grasp on the essentials. After this, keeping plants happy often comes down to intuition. Gardening is, after all, a combination of education and experience. ——➤

Curb Your Enthusiasm

Impulse buying comes easy. But when choosing your plant, be selective. The key way to understand a plant's needs is to find out about its origins. A large majority of houseplants originate from tropical or sub-tropical climates, and will thrive in indoor environments with a minimum of 15°C with some sun. Understanding houseplants' origins provides a safe basis for acclimatizing them to your home.

Essentially, the plants to look for are ones with strong leaves that are not turning yellow at the edges (unless they are meant to). If you are shopping for a particular type, it is a good idea to find out beforehand what the plant looks like at its healthiest.

Good to know: Make sure that the roots are not coming out of the container. This is a sign that the plant has been in the pot for too long and outstayed its welcome. ——●

Rise and Shine

Every plant has unique sunlight requirements, and, as a general rule, the more sunlight a plant receives, the more water it will need. Though doctor's orders for your plant might have called for bags of

sunlight, placing it in front of a south-facing window can burn or wilt its leaves. Keep an eye on how houseplants with high exposure to sunlight are holding up, especially when temperatures begin to rise.

Good to know: When going on a summer vacation, it is safer to move your plants to the center of the room or a spot that garners more indirect sunlight. By the same token, some plants might benefit from being moved to a windowsill during the winter. ——●

Plant Enthusiast Fem Güçlütürk's Holiday Care Tips

1. Dim the sunlight by drawing the curtains
2. For big planters, plastic bottles filled with water can be placed in the soil upside down, so water slowly soaks into the earth
3. Ask a good friend to help out with watering

Room to Breathe

Make It Rain

Overwatering is the most common cause of plant death. While there is no one-size-fits-all rule, finding out how much water your plant requires and how often, either by checking its tag or asking at your local garden shop, is key. When watering, the best way is to do so until water leaks out from the bottom of the pot. For plants in self-draining containers, it is a good idea to check the saucer after a day to see if any water is left over to dispose. If your tap water is chalky, acid-loving plants will appreciate being given bottled water–though it is an expensive option.

Good to know: An easy way to find out whether a plant needs more water is to lift it: a dryer plant will be lighter, whereas a wet one heavier. ——●

When replanting into a new container from the one the plant came in, it is best if the new pot allows water to drain out. Ideally, containers should be the same size as the one the plant was bought in, as this avoids using too much soil and overwatering later on. Material-wise, moisture-saving containers in terracotta, resin, and fiberglass are a safe choice and can be easily matched to glazed saucers or bottom dishes.

Good to know: Plants that need dry roots–such as succulents and herbs–should be potted in self-draining containers, while plants that prefer wet roots–ferns, for example–will do better in closed ones. ——●

I always say start small and build up your confidence, there is nothing worse than spending lots of money and then seeing it all die in front of your eyes.

Isabelle Palmer, The Balcony Gardener

In the Heat of it All

Generally speaking, houseplants of tropical origin require an indoor temperature of between 15°C and 24°C.

Keeping plants away from drafty spots, air conditioners, and central heating systems is vital. The eye-catching fiddle-leaf fig might cover a radiator that is an eyesore, but during the winter being close to central heating will dry them out or kill them. With the heating on, plants will often not require more water but regular misting of the leaves to make up for the lack of humidity.

Good to know: Too little sunlight can lead to plant leaves turning a pale yellow, a condition known as chlorosis. While most commonly caused by lack of sunlight, the yellowing can also be a sign of a nutrient deficiency, pests, over- or under-watering, or come as a result of dusty leaves. —•

17

The Plant Whisperer

Fem Güçlütürk   Istanbul, Turkey

In a crammed, terraced apartment in the Beşiktaş district of Istanbul, Fem Güçlütürk can almost certainly be found watering her plants. Over the years, the plant enthusiast has collected over 1,000 specimens, making her the guest in a home overgrown with wildlife

It was during a trip to Copenhagen that Fem was reintroduced to nature. She and a friend rented a small house that belonged to an artist, charmingly characterized by triangular windows and a low glow of light. Here, the presence of plants awakened a clarity that would inspire the next chapter of her life, one with a bit more clutter than anticipated.

For 12 years Fem was a partner at a brand consulting firm. Moving to the city came with many good things, but also a gradual retreat from the natural world, a connection she soon realized ran deep in her blood.

"As Anatolians we believe that animals and plants have a deep soul. The ability to communicate with plants has been passed down from our ancestors, who lived in direct relationship to the land. It is in our bones," Fem explains. In a turn of fate, the home she bought belonged to a ceramic artist, who left a collection of pots, endemic shrubs, and trees in her care. "My future and destiny came with a sales contract," Fem recalls.

A home with a terrace soon became a non-negotiable. A collection of 20 plants quickly multiplied into hundreds, as did her collection of books on horticulture—

including an encyclopedia of seventeenth-century botanical drawings. A new world had opened its doors, one that is ever-present yet always evolving. "Talking to plants is simple. We all talk too much sometimes; but to learn how to listen is the main issue. To understand plants' needs you have to learn their language, to read the signs without talking in words, but in smell, color, and shape."

When Fem opened a store next to her home in a disused motorcycle garage, her collection only kept growing. Selling one plant meant buying five more; finding a new species meant purchasing at least a couple of its kind. When visitors enter the store they are speechless, awestruck, confused. "'Alice down the rabbit hole' or

'green heaven on earth'—that's what they mostly say. There is an ugly apartment in front of our small cottage. Once you step in, you start to feel our green vibes."

Waking up with the birds at 5:00 or 6:00 in the morning to water the plants, especially during hot summer months, comes with the job. In the afternoon, the game starts again. No one specimen is more interesting than another; to the plant enthusiast, each creature has smart, witty, and wise traits. The wild tobacco plant, for instance, can change the color of its flowers within a day. This protective mechanism attracts insects to lay eggs on its leaves; the plant then changes its pigment again to attract other pollinators to eat their larvae, preventing the leaves

To understand plants' needs you have to learn
their language, to read the signs without talking in words,
but in smell, color, and shape

Fem Güçlütürk

from being eaten. "Who can change their hair color without any help?" Fem asks in amazement.

Before renovating the greenhouse area of her store, Fem spent days and nights observing the daylight patterns of each season. Trees surrounding the building are pruned accordingly. Shelves and tables are moved around almost every week to follow the sun's rays. Although homes in Istanbul are heated to 24°C during the winter out of habit, the temperature in Fem's home and studio is 18°C to best recreate the plants' natural habitat.

Fem has been in botanical gardens and cactus forests around the world, from Sri Lanka to Swaziland, Bolivia to Barcelona, and Mozambique to Marrakesh. At each turn she is impressed by how well nature does on its own, and the ways in which plants communicate through subtle energies and chemistries: turning to a light source with their stems; responding to warmth and cold; sending out defensive chemicals when insects attack. "We often forget about the importance of nature, the fact that we cannot survive without other species, but plants can certainly survive without us. Everyone has the ability to interpret the language of plants if they want to. Look deeper. Create a bond. Examine their daily changes. We often forget that we are nature. It is when we lose our connection to nature that we lose the connection to ourselves." ➜

① Hanging trees by The Joy of Plants ② Living room plants by Haarkon
③ Kitchen window by Lobsters and Swan ④ Kitchen shelf by Lobsters and Swan

26

①

②

③

④

27

③

① Styling by Kråkvik Dorazio ② & ③ Cactus displays at Kaktus København
④ Potted barrel cactus at Kaktus København

④

Bucket-Lights Get the Green Light

Roderick
Vos

's-Hertogenbosch,
The Netherlands

——— Looking to better workers' wellbeing in office environments, the Dutch designer Roderick Vos created an upside-down planter that inspires a positive atmosphere while adding a stylish touch to a sparse room. Constructed out of two 2-mm-thick aluminum buckets that are powder-coated in green, the hanging plant fixtures are outfitted with LED lights. Plants have been shown to benefit overall performance and motivation in the workplace; by emitting oxygen and cleaning the air, they reduce our stress levels and improve memory retention. For Vos and his design team, developing the ideal lamp for their studio brought another benefit; based on their office layout, the team developed a variation on the standard bucket-light model, housing built-in power sockets between the planters. This allows the designers to connect their computers more neatly, taking care of the usual tangle of power cords at their feet. Part office and part showroom, this space is a prime example of a pleasant and productive work enivronment. ———•

In Sebastopol, in California's Sonoma County, a neglected wooden farm has been transformed into an art studio and storage spot for farm equipment. Mork Ulnes Architects took on the design challenge given by the new owners, an art collector and a painter who wanted to combine the farm's agrarian aesthetic with modern sensibilities. After the existing barn was deemed irreparable, the architects chose to invert the barn roof, pitching it to create a sweeping double-height space ideal for the climate-safe storage of artworks and collectibles. The barn wood was reused for exterior cladding. The smaller building features an open concrete kitchen and dining area with a garden landscape that creeps in through the entrance; nicknamed the Amoeba, the space is indefinite in shape, stretching out

The Creeping Landscapes of Meier Road

Casper Mork-Ulnes, Grygoriy Ladigin   Sebastopol, CA, United States

to engulf the landscape. The roof, a construction of exposed wood and scissor-beams, diffuses sunlight to bring in ideal amounts for both plants and people. ➤

Natural Encounters at Atelier Botânico

Carol Nóbrega, Antonio Jotta

São Paulo, Brazil

Atelier Botânico brings nature back into our daily lives with unique terrariums from Carol Nóbrega and Antonio Jotta. What began as a hobby for this design-loving couple blossomed into a business when a growing number of their friends placed personal orders. When Atelier Botânico opened in São Paulo in September 2015, the oddly shaped, charming terrariums found a new home alongside equally fantastic vases and exotic palms. The store's philosophy–the more eccentric the plant or planter the better–makes for an eclectic assemblage of sorts. Inspired by the couple's strolls around Paris' Le Marais district, with its quaint floral shops, Atelier Botânico is enlivened by good design and nature running wild. Vintage reins here, and with time the store's display of indoor plants, flowers, natural curiosities, and living arrangements has grown into something bigger. Today, terrarium-building and flower wreath workshops are held alongside a curated collection of gardening tools, books, and botanical wallpaper. When visitors come in they often feel as if they are being reintroduced to nature, a meeting the owners have happily facilitated. ➤

Bloomage Daydream: Delivering Petals By Pedal

Caroline Stephenson ❧ Berlin, Germany

In Berlin, Caroline Stephenson pedals her way to a greener future. The young florist works by the rules of sustainability in bringing fresh bouquets to doorsteps across the city, which she assembles out of German- or European-grown flowers, and delivers strictly by bicycle. On Tuesdays, Stephenson rises as early as 4 a.m. to head to the local flower market, selecting seasonal blooms for two weekly bouquets that can be ordered through her online shop. Growing up in rural Wales among fresh produce and a house full of plants, Stephenson takes her roots very seriously. She strives to keep her environmental impact low by sourcing a sweet minimum and replenishing flowers throughout the week, while not a single stem goes unused. Bloomage Daydream takes inspiration from David Bowie's *Moonage Daydream*, and the homegrown business reflects an appreciation for the little things. "In this world of plenty," says Stephenson, "it is better to do a few things well. In keeping the bouquet choice to a carefully curated minimum, the wasted stock is minimal, too."

46

Around the Block with The Petaler

Rebekah Northway   San Francisco, CA, United States

●——— The embodiment of flowers on the go, The Petaler is a one-woman floral business run from the back of Rebekah Northway's 1984 AM General. The van might be the eye-catcher of the business, but the floral project within is so much more. Based in San Francisco but originally from Santa Fe, Northway provides everything from fresh weekly arrangements for the home to bouquets for restaurants, offices, and event venues around the city. Some days her van just parks it, transforming into a pop-up shop. Having outgrown her previous wheels, the truck is now big enough to house the branches and longer stems at the center of her creations, while the flowers jump up and down to the rhythm of the road as the old engine sputters. ———➤

Living in a Glass House

Helly Scholten — Rotterdam, The Netherlands

In the name of science, the Scholten family moved into a greenhouse for three years. Despite plenty of ups and downs, they wouldn't trade away a minute

Interior decorator and plant stylist Helly Scholten has always been fascinated by how interiors can influence a dweller's sense of place and wellbeing. Among the many ways that a space can be infused with life, nature is often forgotten about as an easy way to soften appearances and open up a home. Life in the greenhouse, Scholten says, feels like a year-round holiday.

Together with a group of friends, Scholten had previously tried to build an off-the-grid "earth house" in Rotterdam's city center. When met with permit restrictions and difficulties in securing the land, they called off the project. So when word got out that students at the University of Rotterdam were looking for a family to test their first livable greenhouse on, Scholten found the opportunity too good to pass up. Headed by professor A.J. Karssenberg under the Department of Sustainable Building, the project was part of the students' concept house village. "I was in the right spot at the right time with the right person," recalls Scholten. "That does not happen often, but it happened this time."

In June 2015 the family moved into the 135-square-meter greenhouse for a three-year period. In adjusting to their new home, Helly Scholten, her husband Mark de Leeuw, their two daughters, and their dog, are finding life more fulfilling than ever anticipated. A rooftop garden supplies vegetables, fruits, and herbs, while also holding water tanks to store rainwater and irrigate plants. Figs are grown beside the sofa, lemons next to the stove. Frequently, the family experiments with new plants such as indigo; not only edible, the plant can also

be used to extract indigo dye, which the family uses as paint. Practically everything grown in the house is utilized in some way, although buying a plant for purely aesthetic reasons has not lost its charm.

The provision of inexpensive heating and cooling was solved by building the dwelling out of wood and incasing the structure in a greenhouse. Still a test project, life in the glass house is a constant work-in-progress. During the summer, when temperatures rise above 25° C, it gets too hot to spend time on the terrace or balcony. When water spills on the roof, the loam coating on the walls below begins to wash away. Wooden floors permit little privacy, and from spring to autumn nearly two hours a day go into watering plants. The perks, though, easily trump any downside. Even on a dark day, the daylight that bathes the home works like magic. During January and February, being in the greenhouse takes away even the smallest hint of winter depression, while storms and lightening have become all the more spectacular. "We made a new start as a family by living here. I can recommend it to anyone," says Scholten.

The greatest compliment the family gets is that they have inspired people to live along their lines. On social media, where the family regularly posts pictures of their day-to-day experiences and freshly harvested produce, the Scholtens are a model for those looking to become more in-tune with environmentally conscious living. "A picture speaks a thousand words, and this house is one big photography set. When we come home we see an experimental playground."

With people spending 90 percent of their time indoors these days, it is more important than ever to make a home livable. The family's best advice is to make use of edible plants and flowers as decoration, and start sowing with one kind of vegetable, planted in different pots around the home and garden to see which area works best. If a tree can be planted, one that bears fruit to harvest will prove the most rewarding. For those interested in sustainable home building, the Scholtens recommend using natural materials such as wood, loam, straw, and natural paint and oils. On a basic level, keeping windows and doors open strengthens associations to the outdoors.

When these three years of experimental living are up for the Scholten family, they will be ready to move on to the next adventure. Although it will be difficult to part with having a greenhouse, another goal has their attention: "Our next step is to be completely self-providing, to live in a house by the water or on a boat. What we really want is to experience what water does when a person lives right by it." ⟶

Persephone's Tropical Treasures

We Came In Peace (Kim Swift and Andrew Stevens),
floral design in collaboration with One Half Nelson  Los Angeles,
CA, United States

— In Greek mythology, Persephone was the queen of the underworld, daughter of Zeus, and goddess of spring growth. In California, Persephone's is a wandering botanical shop: a Los Angeles-based venture that opens its doors for seasonal editions. Launched in winter 2016, the shop explores nature through the lens of mythology, feminism, and the avant-garde, offering an assortment of rare specimens, plant wares, and sculptural objects. The plants are presented in extravagant and abstract planters, providing an alternative to the friendly flower-shop aesthetic in favor of something otherworldly and mysterious. Ceramic planters, urns, and oddly shaped vessels are matched to eucalyptus, orchids, bamboo, and rare desert specimens. Railings leading up the stairs are covered in thick moss in a style both brutalist and sculptural; unusual Japanese ikebana flower arrangements line the shelves; curated naturalist items sit beneath locked glass cases. Persephone's is a truly tropical treasure trove, blooming for a short time before retreating until the next season. —

TELEPHONESBOTANICA

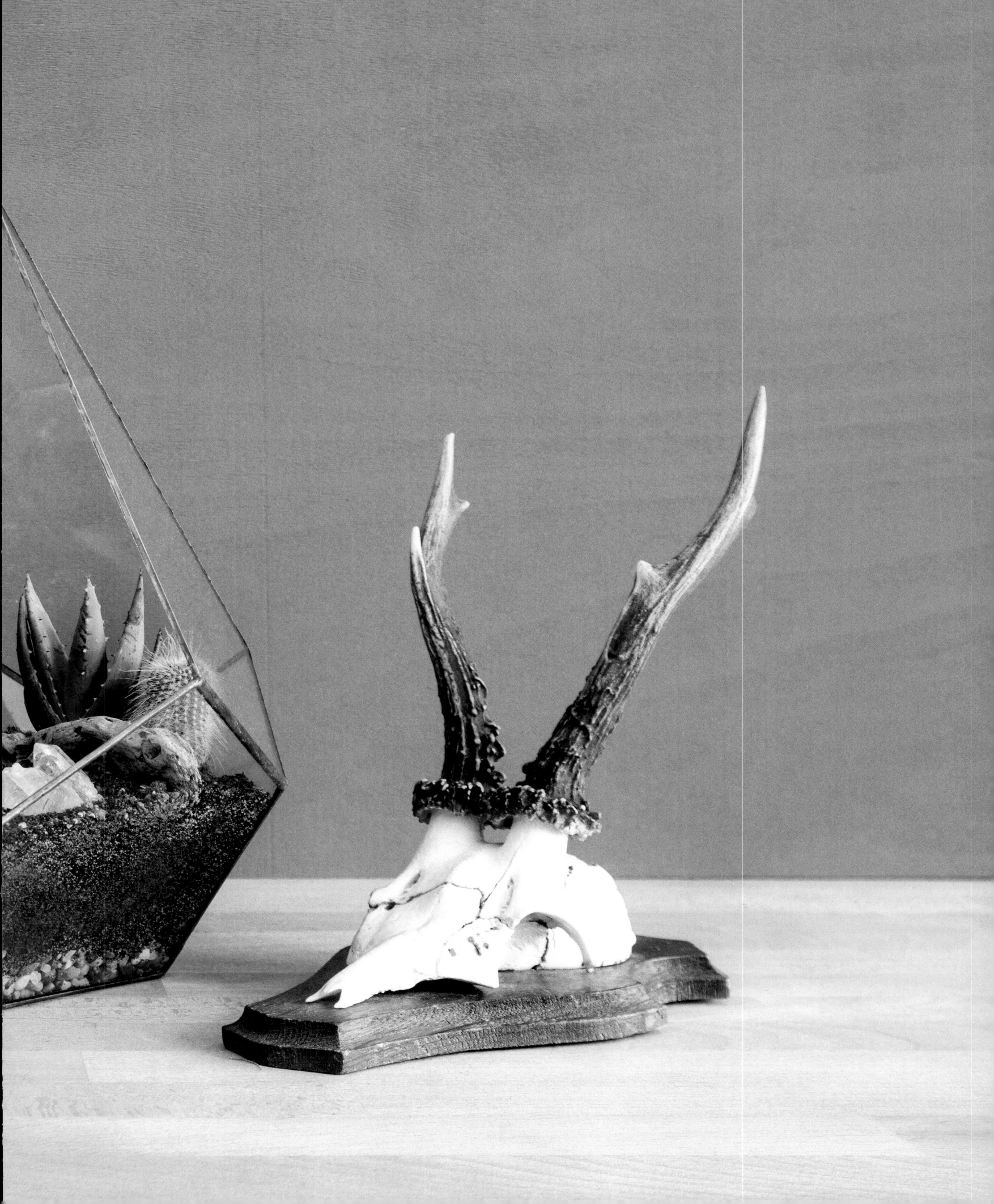

① Greenhouse by Atelier 2+ ② Arizona Collection by mpgmb

At Swallows & Damsons, Romance Is in the Details

Anna Potter 🌱 Sheffield, United Kingdom

◆—— Wild flowers and antiques make a magical combination in Swallows & Damsons, a quaint flower shop and studio set in a perfectly shabby building in Sheffield, England. Nestled between local landmarks and vintage shops, its location presented the ideal combination of creativity and community for founder Anna Potter. Here, her taste for the time-worn and the naturalistic comes to life. An old cash register looks all the more charming in the company of classic botanical illustrations and cabinets chock-full of bouquet ribbons. After working with two of the city's front-running florists, the floral designer decided to specialize in romantic bouquets for both public and private events, with a particular weakness for weddings. Potter's creations enjoy the carefree mingling of wild foliage with bursting chrysanthemums and plump pastel roses, together with foraged branches and berries. Natural materials of wood, terracotta, and copper rein throughout the shop, with the brightness of the blooms against the gray walls waking the space up in winter. ——▶

Getting Your Bearings

Plant placements and styling tips for the balcony, rooftop, and terrace

Climbing Plants

Vines and climbing plants are excellent for both screening and greening balconies—and can safely be planted beside walls or railings. Try a climbing grapevine or an evergreen clematis. ⟶●

Southern Sun

Your balcony's direction will determine which plants will grow well. Having a south-facing balcony will mean frequent watering during summer months. Luckily, more sun also means that growing fruit and vegetables is easy. Try tomatoes, leafy greens, and carrots, dwarf fruit tree varieties and chillies. ⟶●

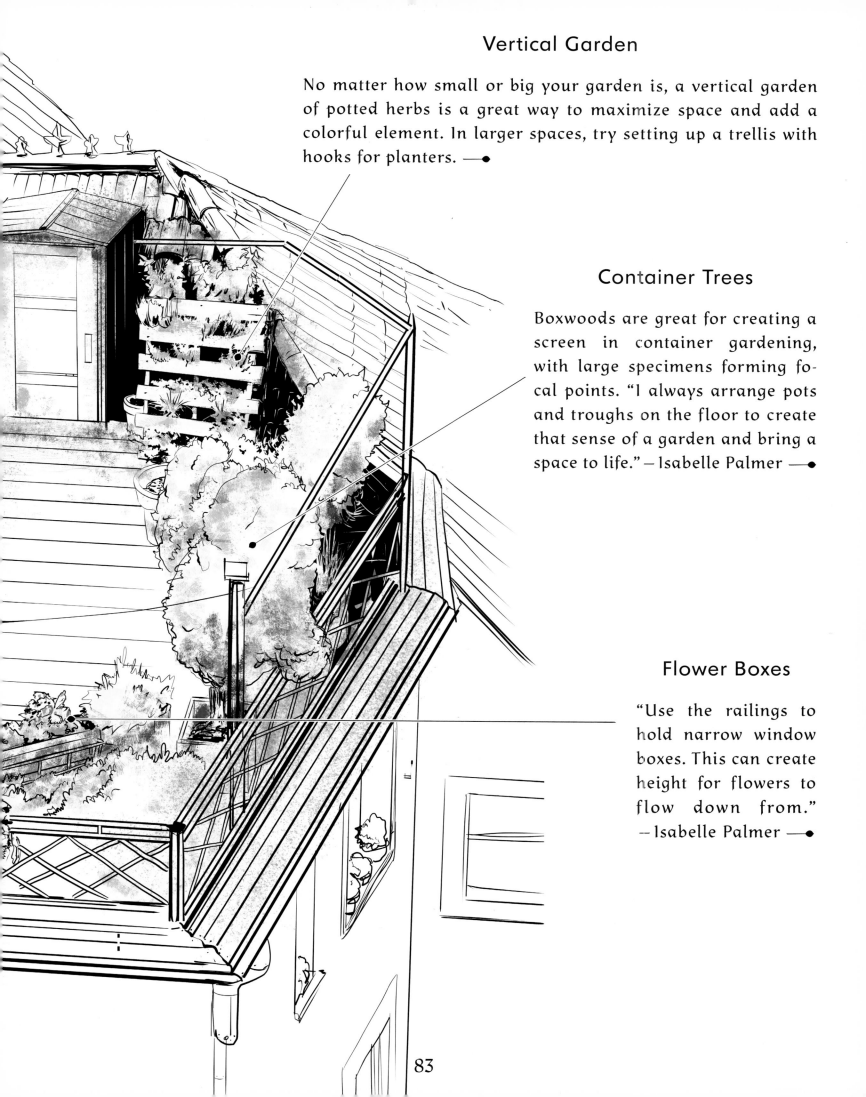

Vertical Garden

No matter how small or big your garden is, a vertical garden of potted herbs is a great way to maximize space and add a colorful element. In larger spaces, try setting up a trellis with hooks for planters. ⟶●

Container Trees

Boxwoods are great for creating a screen in container gardening, with large specimens forming focal points. "I always arrange pots and troughs on the floor to create that sense of a garden and bring a space to life." — Isabelle Palmer ⟶●

Flower Boxes

"Use the railings to hold narrow window boxes. This can create height for flowers to flow down from."
— Isabelle Palmer ⟶●

Tools of the Trade

The limited space of balconies and terraces calls for tools
and containers with an organizational bent

Mix and Match: Big Pots and Containers

City living might restrict garden possibilities, but it does not preclude them altogether. Apartment balconies present enclosed areas that call upon the compositional prowess of gardeners, a skill set that rests upon adept flower and vessel selection.

① Horizontal containers and balcony troughs can be placed neatly along outdoor walls, providing a compact space to display a variety of complementary plants. Their large surface area is also conducive to growing herbs.

② The French-made BACSAC planting bag is a sustainable, lightweight alternative to heavy terracotta and stone planters. Designed to balance water, soil, and air, the geotextile bag employs advanced technology that secures plants against frost and protects fragile roots. Other household bags and sacks can be utilized in a similar way, as long as the material is woven tightly enough to hold water and soil.

③ Trellises provide shade and can be an answer to dwindling garden space. Strawberries are delicious summer climbers, not to forget the ever-faithful rose, which always creates a prominent focal point in any garden. When the dialog between container, plant, and space is carefully considered, balconies can be transformed into beautiful areas that rival any traditional garden. ━━●

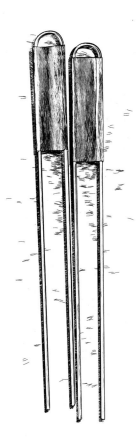

Name Signs

Plants can be hard to identify, especially during their sprouting phases. To keep track of brimming container gardens and the different requirements of each plant, it is a good idea to use name cards. The classic metal peg variety is a subtle complement to balcony gardens, or growers can tap into their creative powers and make their own. ➝●

Vertical Gardens

Running out of space on the balcony? Have an unflattering wall that needs to be covered? Vertical gardens offer a flexible growing method that not only serves practical ends, but also adds a charm of its own to semi-outdoor areas. Considering that the bays rest on top of one another, be sure to place them only in very sunny areas where each level will get its due amount of light. ➝●

Seeds

For the most eager gardeners, seeds are a straightforward way of getting a head start on summer. The packets can be organized in modular storage units, so as to make identification easier when the time comes to plant. Tomatoes, basil, and marigolds are all reliable indoor growers, requiring only a clear path to a south-facing window, fresh potting mix, regular watering, and liquid fertilizer. When the weather gets warmer, seedlings can be tentatively introduced to the outdoors in a process called hardening off. Over a period of a week, each plant should be placed in the elements for a few hours to gradually acclimate to the new environment. ➝●

Scissors and Hand Rake

Having the right tools can be the difference between a garden's success and failure. Using instruments unsuited to the purpose at hand can damage flowers, the risks becoming even more present when dealing with teeming flowerbeds on patios and balconies. For these fragile and involved environments, the sizes of the tools are extremely important, and the higher-quality instruments, though more expensive, are usually more accurate and longer lasting. Garden scissors come in many varieties, from oversized loppers to miniature pruning shears.

① Medium-sized units are particularly suited to terrace gardens with robust plants, like wooden stemmed roses or small trees. On top of the protection provided by gloves, some pairs of scissors offer added security via circular grips that enclose the hand, making them ideal for thorny jobs.

② Smaller varieties of scissors, by contrast, should be used to trim flowers in congested container gardens. Their slightness provides the gardener with the dexterity necessary for navigating tight areas without disrupting other nearby plants.

③ Another valuable tool for flowerbeds is the hand rake. These can be used to clean away fallen foliage in a controlled way, as they are easy to maneuver in confined spaces. One of the most important features of these tools is a strong connection between handle and metal, and choosing a brightly colored instrument is a good idea for the forgetful. ⟶

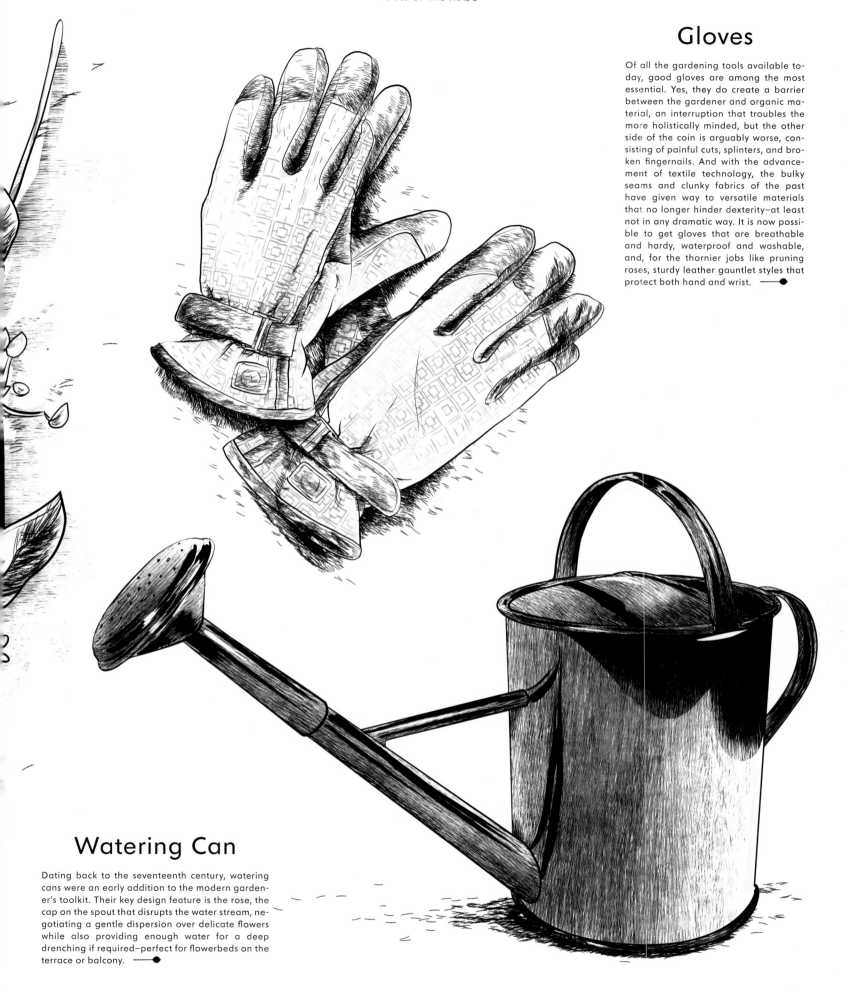

Gloves

Of all the gardening tools available today, good gloves are among the most essential. Yes, they do create a barrier between the gardener and organic material, an interruption that troubles the more holistically minded, but the other side of the coin is arguably worse, consisting of painful cuts, splinters, and broken fingernails. And with the advancement of textile technology, the bulky seams and clunky fabrics of the past have given way to versatile materials that no longer hinder dexterity—at least not in any dramatic way. It is now possible to get gloves that are breathable and hardy, waterproof and washable, and, for the thornier jobs like pruning roses, sturdy leather gauntlet styles that protect both hand and wrist. ——•

Watering Can

Dating back to the seventeenth century, watering cans were an early addition to the modern gardener's toolkit. Their key design feature is the rose, the cap on the spout that disrupts the water stream, negotiating a gentle dispersion over delicate flowers while also providing enough water for a deep drenching if required—perfect for flowerbeds on the terrace or balcony. ——•

Good Things Grow in Small Places

Container plants arranged in transitional spaces act
as mediators between contrasting environments

Strawberries

Fragaria × ananassa

An alluring treat for the senses, strawberries are aromatic, decorative, and delicious. Best grown in summer and spring, the plant is quite resilient and will pro-
mulgate easily, but the fruit is susceptible to insects and requires extra watering.
Runners can simply be pegged into the soil as they sprout, making the plant
ideal for thin pots that sit neatly on balcony railings. These shoots can also be
cut off and placed in a hanging basket; or, if left to grow, they will help the plant
to climb, covering surfaces with lush spreads of leaf and berry. ━━●

Origin Brittany, France · Height Depends on growing method. Individual
plants usually reach 30 cm high · Watering schedule Once a day when
fruiting, or enough to keep the soil damp, and twice a week during the
colder months

Poppies

Papaveraceae

Poppies have become a beloved ornamental feature of many veran-
das and porches. Since they grow well from pots of nearly any size,
they can be easily added to container gardens. Some popular kinds
include the Oriental red, California orange, and the multicolored
Iceland poppy, all of which grow well in full sunlight and dry conditions. Blooming throughout spring and summer, poppy flowers are long
lasting supplements to vibrant and colorful gardens. ━━●

Origin South Asia · Height 30–70 cm
Watering schedule At least once a week

Succulents

(Various)

Otherwise known as fat plants, these juicy specimens find strength in their ability to retain water for long periods of time. Their characteristic plumpness effectively adds contrast to leafy gardens, while full succulent landscapes, emphasized by rock and stone, turn entranceways and terraces into inviting areas redolent of desert oases. One of the best ways to grow succulents is from pots made of concrete, terracotta, or stone, and dry soil and direct sun are the ideal conditions for many of the varied types. ——●

Origin Various · Height Smaller varieties can be just a few centimeters high, while larger cacti like the saguaro can reach 12 – 18 m · Watering schedule Between once per week and once per month, depending on the size of the container and plant type

Snapdragon

Antirrhinum

The snapdragon's colors range across a rich spectrum. Vivid reds, snappy oranges, and delicate, creamy pastels work to imbue gardens with enduring pockets of life. The plant thrives in the cooler temperatures of spring and autumn, and in warmer climates it has even been known to overwinter. Well-drained pots kept in partial shade give it the best chance of surviving past its first year, but it can also be grown out of extremely dry spots like rock walls. ⟶●

Origin Southern Europe and the Mediterranean · Height Smaller plants range from 15–20 cm, and larger ones from 75–120 cm
Watering schedule Frequently over summer, and less often through spring and autumn

Lavender

Lavandula

The soothing fragrance of lavender and its many therapeutic uses have seen it become a staple in gardens all over the world. The distinct silver, green, and purple coloring brightens up transitional spaces while infusing them with a welcoming scent, a quality that also enhances the effectiveness of herb gardens. As a perennial, maintenance is simple, consisting of full sun, drained soil, and pruning to spur growth. Suitable to a wide variety of pots, especially long and thin planters, it can be added to balconies and terraces of any size. ⟶●

Origin The Mediterranean, Middle East, and India
Height Dependent on growing method. A shrub is usually 30–90 cm high
Watering schedule Only when the soil is dry

Fig

Ficus carica

As one of the first known cultivated crops, the fig's toughness has propelled it through the long history of agriculture. Full sunlight and well-drained soil are convenient catalysts for sustained growth, conditions that are found in surplus on sun-drenched balconies and terraces during the summer. The tropical appearance of the tree, with its lobed dark green leaves and radiant purple fruit, also delivers an ornamental elevation to these semi-outdoor areas, a beauty that comes at little cost to the gardener. ●

Origin The Middle East and Western Asia · Height 7–10 m
Watering schedule Regularly water young plants. Once established, a thorough watering once every week or two is enough

Tomato

Solanum lycopersicum

The many varieties of the tomato plant have been traced back to Mesoamerica. Besides their use as a cooking ingredient, some ancient cultures found spiritual powers in the seeds of the plant. Surviving today as a core element of modern kitchens, domestic gardeners have become fascinated with producing the fruit–yes, fruit, not vegetable. The standard types need to be staked to support the heavy fruit, while varieties like the cherry tomato grow well in small pots or hanging baskets. ●

Origin South and Central America ·
Height 1–3 m
Watering schedule Twice a week, or often enough to keep the soil damp

91

An Elevated State

From neglected nook to revered room:
Essential know-how to
transform the balcony into a garden

If having a balcony is not enough to get your heart racing, consider the ideal set-up and creative solutions for your space. Perhaps this is produce-focused, with tomato stakes and containers growing rocket and beetroot, and maybe berries. Or maybe it is a corner to unwind, a go-to vertical garden of potted herbs, or a setup of chairs around a bistro table, ready to entertain. Imagining a landscape in the city can be difficult, but with the addition of an evergreen, the privacy of thick bamboo, and annual flowers, you're already there. ——●

Fear of Heights

Elevated locations are a pressure point for plants. The elements rush in to sweep petals off their feet and the seasons quickly change. Even in places where the cold spell is nowhere in sight and magnolias are endlessly in bloom, the balcony garden can be an exotic undertaking.

But potential lurks in (and on) the smallest of outposts, so gardeners need to be ruthless in their undertaking, making every inch count. Forget about what is in bloom at the nursery—every space has its own demands. Everything from the amount of exposure to wind, sun, and heat to the facing direction and local climate will impact the growth of your plants.

Gardeners need to be mindful of what they want and what is achievable. Indeed, the challenge often lies in creating an alchemy between the in- and outdoors. But with a little know-how and time, the rewards of engaging with your space will prove rich and enduring. ——●

Settling In

To promote their growth, newly bought plants should be carefully re-potted from their original containers, especially if roots are sticking out. Make sure the container is just about the same size as the original, then water and place in a shady spot until the plant settles into its new home. —•

Winds of Change

Balconies and rooftops are microclimates, and wind and storms are balcony plants' biggest enemies. Broken limbs, dried-out soil, and tipped-over planters are common events in the summer, with freezing and desiccating harming plants during the winter. Installing a screen, such as panels attached to a framework of scaffolding poles, can limit this exposure. Further to this, consider whether and how much of the space offers partial sunlight, partial shade, and full shade. Additionally, take note of indirect sunlight, whether it is coming in through tree leaves or bouncing off a building, before deciding on what to plant and grow. —•

Step-by-Step Potting

1. To prep for potting, water your plant thoroughly a day before you begin
2. Carefully turn the plant upside down and tap the container to release roots
3. Trim roots back if they are circling the plant, pruning dead or long roots
4. Fill your new planter with a base layer of new potting mix, sit the plant atop, and secure the plant by surrounding it with more soil
5. Water well and allow to drain

Seasonal Solutions

Keeping a base of evergreens will keep your balcony looking good all year round; though to be safe, avoid buying plants that are unsuited to your local climate. Many plants can also be moved indoors during the winter and kept near your brightest windows. If you are looking to grow edibles in colder climates, choose varieties that grow quickly, such as salad greens, radishes, and carrots. —•

My advice is always to begin by looking at your favorite color, even if you don't have a favorite plant—then move onto heights.

Isabelle Palmer, The Balcony Gardener

Dirt on Your Hands

Working with soil can put many people off gardening. The idea of providing plants with the right amount of minerals and nutrients can seem distant in a city context. Anything being planted will require potting mix, though. Annuals—including vegetables, flowers, and fruit—work well with a general soilless organic potting mix, while bigger, longer-living bushes and fruit trees should be potted in a soil-based mix, which slowly releases nutrients. Mixes can be enriched with organic fertilizer.

Good to know: Hydrogel crystals are an excellent addition to your balcony plants' potting mix, as they absorb excess water and prevent plants from drying out, which is helpful for windy balconies. ———•

Nurture Nature

No matter how neatly potted your plants may be, insects are bound to make an appearance. To best tackle the situation, working with nature, and understanding that a pest-predator balance can be beneficial is key. Flowering container herbs attract predator insects, while a birdbath can also encourage insects and birds. The more nurturing you are towards your plants (while minimizing the use of pesticides), the more your garden will thrive. If slugs are a problem, placing wool pellets or cups of beer in the soil is a good way to collect them. When containers are close together, it is important to act quickly, as pests can quickly be transported from plant to plant.

Good to know: Hedges make superb bird and insect attractions, providing space for creatures to take cover, while fruit and berry trees and shrubs can act as feeding spots for wildlife. ———•

Water, Water

To make life easier on the balcony, connecting a hose will be a lot quicker than a watering can. Drip irrigation systems with a timer are a good way for staying on top of watering routines or when away from home. On rooftops, collecting rainwater in a rain barrel will save a lot of heavy lifting. Planters with built-in reservoirs will keep thirsty plants such as tomatoes and zucchini happy for several days. ———•

Architect Nathalie Wolberg on creating an alchemy between the in- and outdoors:

1. Extend the color of your walls from in- to outdoors, like we did from the kitchen to the garden
2. Incorporate plants in the indoor area closest to your garden
3. Remove visual barriers to the outside by installing large windows and sliding doors
4. Place your plants right up against the glass to give the feeling of being confronted by nature

94

Growing Up

For larger outdoor areas and rooftops, the addition of taller and denser trees, shrubs, and bushes can take a space up a notch. Providing lasting greenery and privacy, compact-growing plants such as boxwood come in many varieties, from the classic European olive-green kind to Japanese varieties that turn bronze in colder months. Incredibly versatile by nature, boxwoods are suitable for screening, as container gardens, and for formal setups, hedges, and mixed planters. They also respond well to pruning, and are generally easy to grow for their resistance to sun or shade. Younger plants need to be kept in shape more often to encourage denser growth, but winter is generally the ideal time for pruning. ──●

Farm-to-Table Fever

Start small by growing easy herbs, such as parsley, chives, and mint (though mint should be kept in its own container to not take over the pot). Strawberries and edible flowers also make a simple beginning and can be incorporated into everyday cooking. For more complex produce, try carrots, potatoes, beans, and chillies. ──●

95

Suntraps and Sensibilities

Isabelle Palmer   London, United Kingdom

An expert in balcony gardening, Isabelle Palmer lives an elevated life between the rooftops and the sky

Countless city dwellers who at first so diligently look for a home with a balcony all ask themselves the same question: Where to start? In London, Isabelle Palmer has made a business out of transforming small garden spaces into urban oases. Her own empty balcony and desire for a green retreat during the dog days of summer in the city drove her self-taught gardening career.

The Balcony Gardener offers no-nonsense, easily digestible advice for the novice gardener. Taking inspiration from her home's modern interiors and two balconies, Palmer offers ready-made services such as window boxes, as well as comprehensive bespoke design assistance. Outside of her office, a small terrace makes the perfect suntrap. Wall spaces and the tiniest of ledges are alive with greenery and stacked with vertical planters, leaving room to pull out a table and

chairs when the weather suits. Just off the living room, a second balcony serves as a visual paradise, decorated with vintage-style plants in modern dark planters that reflect the dark walls of Palmer's living room. Here, scented plants bring the space to life, attracting bees and butterflies that keep her petite outpost buzzing during the summer.

Palmer always tells new gardeners to build confidence by starting small, with three to five pots. As she says, "There is nothing worse than spending a lot of money to watch your garden die." Using flowers and evergreens will provide a good mix to see you through the seasons, while purchasing bigger pots will give plants all the more space to grow and flourish. "I love making an area overflow with flora and fauna to lead the eye towards green lushness," says Palmer. To further maximize space, railings can be used to hold narrow window boxes; hanging wall planters can add height and instill privacy; pots and troughs can be arranged on the floor for an outside garden feel.

The garden closest to Palmer's heart is at London's Ham Yard Hotel. Located on the fourth floor, this kitchen garden grows everything from strawberries, broccoli, and gooseberries during the summer to herbs throughout the year. Majestic olive trees stand beside apple trees with bending branches, all producing plentiful produce that features in the hotel's dishes and cocktails. "I'm

totally in awe of this garden and can't believe it's there so high up above London," Palmer says. For beginner gardeners looking to grow herbs, parsley, chives, and mint are easy to look after, while more advanced growers might try thyme, bay laurel, and rosemary, which will last all year round. All these, Palmer says, make wonderful additions to everyday cooking.

Undoubtedly, maintaining a balcony, terrace, or rooftop garden in an urban environment can be tricky. "It's normally very windy if you live up high. Not only do you need to be sure everything is well secured, but the wind can also damage plants and increase transpiration, causing them to dry out more quickly," Palmer stresses. These "up in the air" gardens will therefore require more regular watering than those on the ground. "They rely on you for water and food. This is a big challenge, and the one I think is most people's downfall." At the height of summer Palmer fertilizes her plants every

two weeks, but because there is no fertilizer running off into the ground, she uses half the concentration instructed for container plants. Moisture-control soil can also help plants grow in elevated environments by retaining water.

Palmer describes the style of her gardens as modern, uncluttered, and pared back. "I try to use my interior as a guide, whether it is a key color that comes up again in my planting or a particular ornament. I then use these colors in a scheme, creating a fluidity between the two spaces." The incorporation of vivid tropical plants, too, adds dramatic effect, such as the fatsia japonica, agave, gingko biloba, yucca, and cordyline—her list goes on and on. "My advice is always to begin by looking at your favorite color, even if you don't have a favorite plant—then move onto heights." One of her favorite things about balconies is eyeing these sky-high jewels of greenery from the street. This, Palmer says, is one of the most charming ways to liven up a city. ➡

Gang and the Wool:
On the Makings of a Poem

Manuela Sosa　　🌱　　Barcelona, Spain

In the Vallvidrera neighborhood of Barcelona, a small greenhouse flower business finds perfection in the simple things. Bridal bouquets and wedding decor are Gang and the Wool's specialty; always incorporating something spontaneous, they play with the varied textures of fresh petals, twigs, and dried leaves. Owner and florist Manuela Sosa compares the artistic process of composing her bouquets to that of a poem, evoking emotions with each element. Sourcing fresh flowers from the world's largest market in Aalsmeer, the Netherlands, Sosa's Mediterranean aesthetic is nonetheless clear in her finished parcels. The florist opens the doors of her little workspace for small dinner parties, workshops, and photo shoots, where attention to detail brings this delightful oasis to life. A simple vase of clipped flowers or a bunch of herbs in the house is a reward, says Sosa, as the combination, arrangement, and result looks alive. ━━▶

Paris, Texas, Antwerp

Nathalie Wolberg and Tim Stokes Antwerp, Belgium

A house in Antwerp that switches between a private home and a public exhibition space, with nature sprouting up everywhere in between

When French architect Nathalie Wolberg and Texan artist Tim Stokes moved to Antwerp, a neglected warehouse near the port and the city's former red-light district became the perfect blank canvas for their new home. The couple needed room to dedicate to their art and architecture workspaces, but ambition soon gave way to adjoining public exhibition rooms and convivial areas for artists to gather.

When the couple first toured the property, it had been untouched since the 1960s; the only view the outdoor area offered was of towering gray buildings. But in the home's rough edges, skylights, and wide-open spaces was potential that took an architect's eye to unravel. The completed space comes together in a mixture of minerals, featuring concrete floors and ceilings,

brick walls, and plenty of light, incorporating plants to balance out the building's industrial identity. The first floor features a 100-square-meter apartment, while the ground floor combines an exhibition space, three studios, and a social kitchen area over five times the first floor's size. Here, two indoor greenhouses make a unique addition, each ecological habitat a tropical world of its own.

As the creative couple spend about 90 percent of their time in their studios, a sense of openness throughout the property was paramount. The exotic outside garden provides a fulfilling escape from the gray weather and city. Inside, an assortment of small cacti and succulents have taken residence: "We like them for their graphic quality, the warmth they bring from their origins," says Wolberg. The greenhouses were a very

The real value of the garden comes from the sights, sounds, and smells that come along with it, and the reward of being able to stop and reflect on it during the course of the day.

Nathalie Wolberg

Belgian inspiration, a country where fields are scattered with designated vegetation zones. In the kitchen, an airy Dracaena marginata, known as the dragon plant, emerges from a cut-out round in the floor; in the studio, the fragile body of an Albizia tree contrasts the loud interiors and chunky patches of color.

Each area has its own unique design, creating a dynamic and joyful feeling throughout the home. Intimate, cocooned partitions are colored in bright blocks, playing with spatial arrangements and opening new rooms for inspiration. Walls are dipped in an exotic shade of mustard-yellow. A dry riverbed flows through the middle of the outdoor garden, with the warm backdrop of the yellow wall reappearing. "The key to achieving an alchemy between the inside and outdoors is to create a continuity between the two elements," Wolberg says. "To do this we used the same color on

the walls in the studio, kitchen, and garden, so that the result looks like one wall without interruption." Following this thread, giant windows and a sliding glass door remove any visual barriers to the outside, and plants are placed against the glass to create a continuous transition into nature.

While finding a green retreat in an urban center can be difficult, Wolberg and Stokes overcame this obstacle by creating a dense tropical garden that softens the industrial surroundings. Though the garden may be small at 50-square-meters, it still allows onlookers to visually get lost in it. "Saturate your home with plants and it will come to life—and the birds will come too!" says Wolberg. "The real value of the garden comes from the sights, sounds, and smells that come along with it, and the reward of being able to stop and reflect on it during the course of the day." ——▶

Venice House: Indoors, Outdoors and In-Between

Sebastian Mariscal Studio  Venice Beach, CA, United States

●—— The designers and developers behind Sebastian Mariscal Studio have taken an organic approach to the restructuring of this 1920s bungalow in Venice Beach, California. Their concept allows every indoor room of the home to correspond with an outdoor space, such as the courtyard, roof garden, patio, or deck. In creating harmonious transitions from the inside to the outside, human interactions as well as space and energy reduction were taken into account. The mature trees on-site, including a 12-m-tall pine tree, a California live oak, and a magnolia, were a huge draw to the property, and were incorporated into the design. Both Southern California's outdoor lifestyle and its climate certainly had an airy influence as well. ——●

Firma Casa's Vertical Habitat

Artistic Project: Fernando and Humberto Campana,
Architecture: SuperLimão Studio

São Paulo,
Brazil

Reopened in 2012 after a full renovation, the Firma Casa design gallery has become a show-stopping piece of design in itself. Founded in 1996 by Sonia Diniz Bernardini, Firma Casa promotes and supports young Brazilian designers focussing on furniture design. Its stunning façade is made up of 9,000 green seedlings planted in 3,500 vases, coupled with simple steel elements that emphasize an industrial-modern aesthetic. Brazilian designers Fernando and Huberto Campana suggested the green wall and the incorporation of snake plants—Espada-de-São-Jorge, as they are known in Brazil—while the architects at Super-Limão Studio created the "vase" planters out of aluminum mounted on a wire grid. The gallery holds a 76-square-meter exhibition space for limited edition pieces, while in the larger showroom, brands such as Zanotta, Edra, Baleri, and Estudio Campana take residency.

At Sun Path House, a Conversation with the Moon

Studio Christian Wassmann — Miami Beach, FL, United States

●—— Designed to follow the path of the Miami sun, this concrete residence brings the dream of tree-house living to fruition. Both functional and sculptural, the sturdy home was built as an extension to a renovated 1930s bungalow. Featuring a slanted spine that holds a spiral staircase and pizza oven, the home curves upwards across three stories. The result, architect Christian Wassmann says, is based on a dialog between the original house and the cosmos. Surrounded by palm trees, the home's glass exterior is delicately planted with fire vines at its base and passion vines on its roof. The year-round outdoor-living ethos is further accentuated by an outside grill, a kitchen counter made of Carrara marble, and an outdoor shower, with all elements incorporated into the building's concrete exterior. On the rooftop sundeck, the architects constructed a wall in the precise shape of the sun's path in the summer solstice, transforming the home into a sun-worshiping temple of sorts. This rooftop wall also blocks the wind, making room for solitude and serenity under the open sky. ——●

Getting Your Bearings

Plant placements
and styling
tips for the
outdoor garden

Vegetable Patch

Starting a vegetable garden close to the
house makes it easier to harvest produce.
Look for a sunny spot, ideally one that is
a little elevated to avoid flooding. ➞

Garden Shed

Keeping a garden shed is a great way to
hide bulky tools and keep them dry. Often it is convenient to have the shed close
to a water supply—but make sure you are
not covering the most fertile soil. ➞

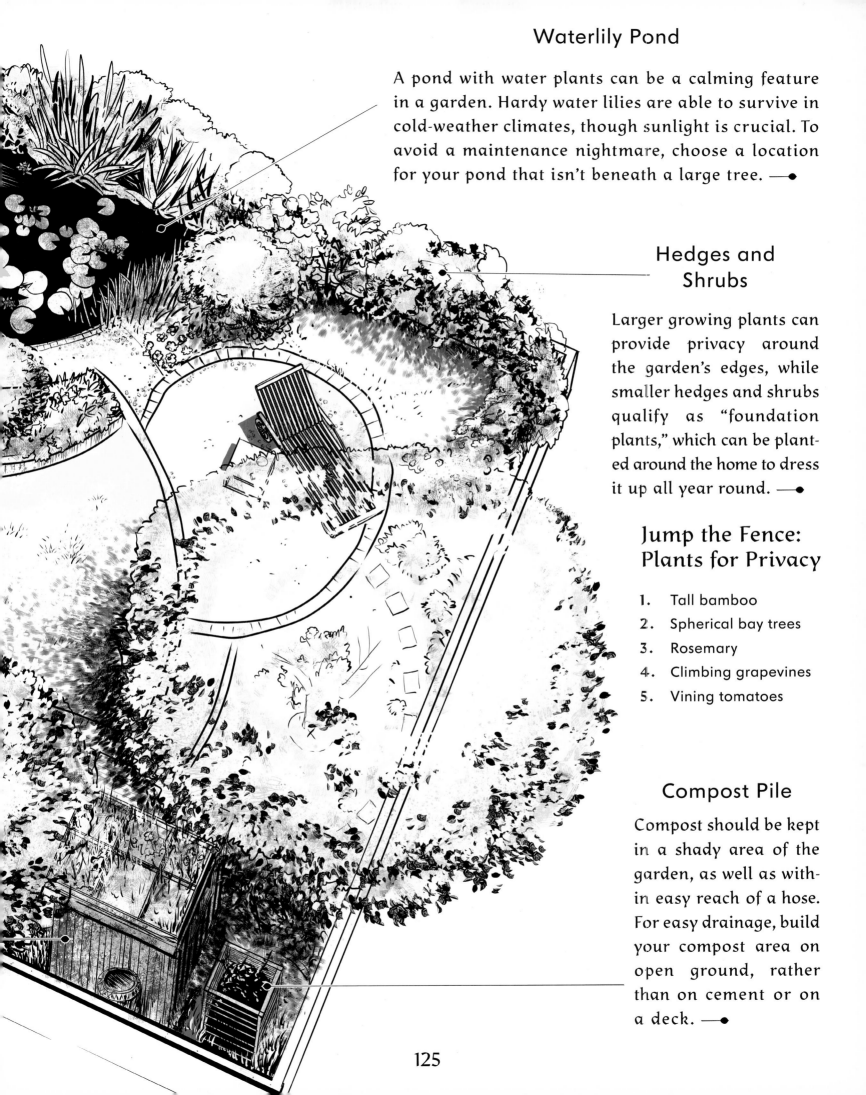

Waterlily Pond

A pond with water plants can be a calming feature in a garden. Hardy water lilies are able to survive in cold-weather climates, though sunlight is crucial. To avoid a maintenance nightmare, choose a location for your pond that isn't beneath a large tree.

Hedges and Shrubs

Larger growing plants can provide privacy around the garden's edges, while smaller hedges and shrubs qualify as "foundation plants," which can be planted around the home to dress it up all year round.

Jump the Fence: Plants for Privacy

1. Tall bamboo
2. Spherical bay trees
3. Rosemary
4. Climbing grapevines
5. Vining tomatoes

Compost Pile

Compost should be kept in a shady area of the garden, as well as within easy reach of a hose. For easy drainage, build your compost area on open ground, rather than on cement or on a deck.

Turning a New Leaf

Capable of standing up to the elements, outdoor plants
that are tough, lush and rewarding to grow

Ornamental Grasses

(Various)

In spacious gardens, ornamental grass acts as a mediator between di-
vergent plants, lending the habitat a general coherence. True grasses,
sedges, rushes, and cats'-tails are some of the most popular varieties,
and, once established, they are very easy to maintain. In most cases,
ornamental grasses are durable perennials, keeping gardens fresh and
interesting as they transform through the seasons. They are uplifting
additions to succulent gardens in particular, as their continual move-
ment offsets an otherwise stable environment. ●

Origin Many species, like true grasses, date back to the
Cretaceous period · Height Smaller varieties are 20 cm,
and larger types can reach 5 m high · Watering schedule Water
often after planting, and later only in periods of drought

Apple Tree

Malus domestica

Of the many fruit plants that can be grown domes-
tically, apple trees are among the simplest to
maintain. Types of trees should be chosen depending on fruit type, which can be roughly split into
two categories: cooking or eating. Some varieties
can certainly suit both purposes. Saplings are the
best starting point for a productive tree, and
planting these in a windless, sunny spot gives them
a better chance of long-term survival. ●

Origin Central Asia · Height Most types grow to
approximately 6 m high · Watering schedule During dry
periods and more often throughout fruiting

Fern

Polypodiopsida

With their soft branched stems and curled fronds, ferns recall a mysterious, prehistoric age of flora. Some species date back as far as the Devonian period; others have remained unchanged over millions of years, like the Osmunda claytoniana, or interrupted fern. Shaded nooks under evergreen trees are ideal points for growth, as the mulch and tree roots provide the kind of spacing and drainage necessary for delicate fern roots. Swaying in communion with the breeze, they imbue gardens with the atmosphere of a forgotten forest, wild and majestic. ━━●

Origin Devonian period · Height Small varieties can be under 1 cm, and larger types range between 10-25 m high · Watering schedule Regularly enough so the soil does not dry out. Spray mist onto the stems

Pumpkin

Cucurbita pepo

From soups and pies to Halloween's jack-o'-lanterns, pumpkins have a variety of uses, featuring prominently in festivals and traditional events. Given their size, spacious vegetable gardens are a prerequisite for comfortable growth, but miniature varieties can be planted in smaller patches, too. Frost must be absolutely avoided, but the vined plants need 75 to 100 days to grow, meaning the best time to plant them is directly after winter when the ground is warm. ━━●

Origin North America · Height 30-90 cm
Watering schedule Frequently when first planted, then once a week

Hydrangea

Hydrangeaceae

Instantly recognizable by their lavish, showy flowers, hydrangeas are an easy-care go-to for gardens that need a little brightening up. Aside from their enchanting appearance, the Hydrangea serrata variety makes a sweet tea, which, in Japan on April 8, is used to celebrate Buddha's birth. The most advantageous time to plant is in spring or fall, preferably away from gusty winds and continual sunlight. To prevent stem breakages, large shrubs must be monitored and pruned as they grow. ———●

Origin South and East Asia and the Americas
Height 1-3 m · Watering schedule One a week, or more often in hot weather

Elderflower

Sambucus nigra

The current elderflower soft drink sensation is a renaissance, not a novelty. The plant's use as a cordial has a long and ingrained history in Northern Europe that dates back to Roman times. In addition to producing the flowers for these drink infusions, the deciduous elder tree also spawns black berries, which are mildly poisonous and need to be boiled before eating. These berries can be used for many things, like the German Fliederbeersuppe and elderberry wine. When in bloom, the tree is showered in an intricate display of white flowers, periodically illuminating garden corners. ———●

Origin Europe, North America, and Asia
Height 6 m · Watering schedule Saplings must be kept damp, and older trees care for themselves

128

Rose

Rosa

Despite its thorns, or maybe because of them, the rose has become closely aligned with romanticism. Bred over centuries, the woody perennial has over 100 different species and many thousands of cultivars, nearly all of which are shrubs with the ability to climb. Careful pruning and regular watering are essential components for healthy growth, and the growing site should have at least six hours of sun per day. They are perfect plants to take cuttings from to decorate the interior of the home, or to give away to the appropriate person. ⟶●

Origin Asia, Europe, North America, and Northwest Africa · Height Climbers can reach up to 7 m high
Watering schedule A thorough watering once per week when growing

Of Flavor and Fragrance

Whether for culinary, medicinal or aesthetic
purposes, herbs award depth, texture and contrast
to their environments and varied uses

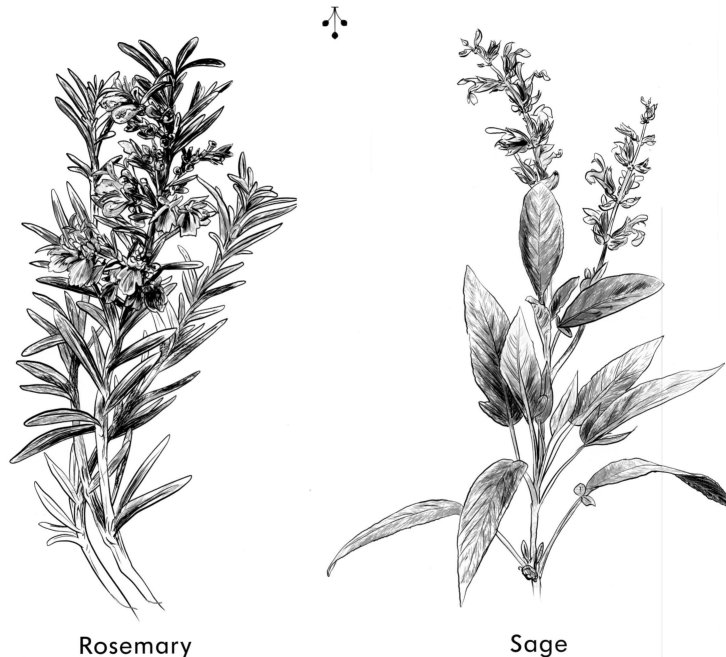

Rosemary

Rosmarinus officinalis

This low-maintenance plant grows wonderfully in warmer zones, and in colder
temperatures, should be transplanted and brought indoors. Requiring six to eight
hours of sunlight a day, rosemary plants won't mind drying out a little in between
being watered. Its piney fragrance makes it an important culinary herb, while its
flowers contain an acid that is both antibacterial and an antioxidant, commonly
used to make essential oils. ➝●

Origin Mediterranean regions

Sage

Salvia officinalis

Best grown from cuttings from another plant, sage is laced with an intensity that
just requires a pinch to take a dish to the next level. Unlike other herb plants, the
medicinal flavor of sage intensifies as its leaves grow bigger, growing well in a
variety of temperatures in well-drained soil. Propagated from cuttings, roots will
grow within six weeks. ➝●

Origin Mediterranean regions

Laurel

Laurus nobilis

Laurel, also called bay leaf or sweet bay, has long held a reputation as a medicinal herb, highly regarded by both the Romans and Greeks as a symbol of peace and wisdom. With leaves rich in Vitamin-C, laurel is commonly used to flavor stews and soups. As a hot-weather herb, laurel retains moisture and flavor, even after dried for several months. ──●

Origin **Mediterranean regions**

Parsley

Petroselinum crispum

More than a garnish, parsley is a classic summer herb used abundantly in cuisines across Greece, Turkey, the Middle East and North Africa. Its volatile oils have shown to provide health benefits, used medicinally prior to being a consumed food. Curly parsley and flat-leaf parsley are the two main varieties, which the latter is characterized by a stronger flavor profile. ──●

Origin **Mediterranean regions**

Mint

Mentha

One of the easiest herbs to grow, mint will thrive in a container or home garden, though ideally on its own, as its roots are very invasive. Mint sprigs should be harvested before the plant flowers, which can be used daily for everything from teas to cooking, making a great palate cleanser. Try freezing mint leaves in an ice cube tray for an instant summer reminder. ──●

Origin **Mediterranean regions**

Cilantro

Coriandrum sativum

Also called coriander after its seeds (its leaves are called cilantro), the plant grows in cooler weather of spring and during the fall. Growing from seedlings will come easy, especially in full sun and well-drained soil. Leaves can be stored in freezer bags, or dried, by hanging them in a warm location before storing them in a re-sealable bag. ──●

Origin **Southern Europe, northern Africa**

Thyme

Thymus vulgaris

A perennial shrub with curved, fragrant leaves, thyme is packed with nutrients, minerals, and vitamins, awarding an aromatic flavor to Mediterranean dishes. With over 350 species, basil is part of the mint family of plants, and will easily grow in sun-splashed locations. ──●

Origin **Southern Europe and Mediterranean regions**

Basil

Ocimum basilicum

While the most commonly cultivated verities include sweet basil and Genovese basil, this easy-to-grow herb comes in countless lesser-known varieties including Thai, lemon, globe and cinnamon. Used for salads, cocktails, syrups and much more, there is hardly no excuse not to grow this leafy green, which will quickly sprout from seed with moist soil and plenty of sunlight. ──●

Origin **India**

Tools of the Trade

Dig, cut, scoop: The utensils to prune away
your gardening problems

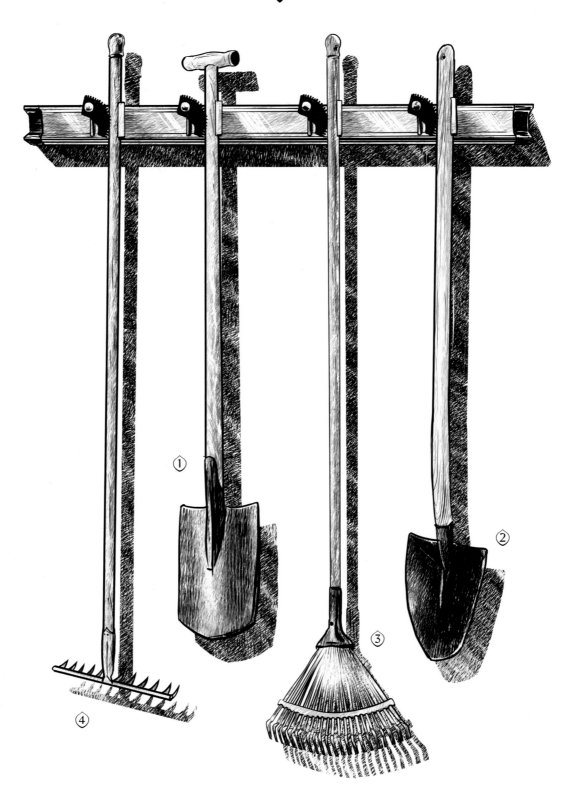

The Fantastic Four

Today the names spade and shovel are often used interchangeably, but they remain distinct instruments for different purposes. ① The spade has a straight blade, its sharp edge and linear dimensions enabling soil to be easily pierced at an optimum angle. Best used on stubborn terrain, it is the instrument of choice when digging new flowerbeds. Traditionally, ② the shovel is more a transporter than a digger. The scooped, broad-bottomed blade allows dirt and other fine materials to be cleanly moved around. Similarly, ③ the fan rake and ④ bow rake are different yet often conflated tools. Both can rake up garden debris and foliage, but only the bow rake, with its sturdy tines, should be used to loosen compacted soil, spread mulch, and level off planting areas.

Handheld tools increase accuracy in confined spaces. ⑤ The hand hoe, for instance, is for a precise method of clearing new space in an existing flowerbed. One of the more rare handheld garden tools, ⑥ the dibbler, usually made of solid wood, is a pointed instrument that is drilled into the ground, creating holes for seeds and small bulbs. ⑦ The weeding tool, another fairly uncommon instrument, comes in a variety of shapes and sizes, but the most useful are the thin, pointed varieties that allow gardeners to get underneath pesky invaders. And where would a gardener be without their trusty ⑧ pruners? These tools can be used to trim anything from roses to thick branches. ➤

Garden Twine

Many varieties of plants need training and support as they grow. From fastening sensitive clematis vines to a trellis, to straightening a young sapling, a hardy, durable twine is all a gardener needs. As the supported plants grow, the string must be monitored to ensure it does not cut into the stems. ➤

Garden Hose

The garden hose is a deceptively complex instrument. Usually made of synthetically extruded rubber or soft plastic, the interior piping is formed by webbed fibers, giving the hose the strength required to channel pressurized water. In winding gardens, these durable materials enable the hose to be pulled and rubbed against pots and trees without disrupting water flow, and the more rigid hoses are resistant to the annoying problem of knotting. Wall-mounted hose reels keep the serpentine tool organized, and portable varieties aid the gardener's mobility. Multipurpose sprayers, with settings that range from powerful jets to light sprinklers, are a helpful accessory that bends water flow to the grower's varying needs. ⬤

Wheelbarrow

Gardening is hard work, particularly when it comes to planting season. Wheelbarrows are relatively effortless ways to transport giant bags of potting mix and fertilizer, as well as being handy tools for collecting and removing garbage from the garden. ⬤

Raised Bed

Otherwise known as garden boxes, these outdoor containers offer succinct ways to present flowers, herbs, and vegetables. Their many benefits include the barrier they put between plants and pests, increased drainage, less chance of soil compaction, and protection from creeping weeds. Gardeners themselves also benefit from the height of the boxes, which helps to mediate the physical toll of gardening. Wood is a common choice of material for these beds, infusing gardens with a rustic atmosphere as it ages. ⬤

Lawnmower

A carefully trimmed lawn is the ultimate complement to a blooming garden. Ride-on models and the standard push mowers are quick and easy methods to cut grass, but their noisy motors erase any trace of garden tranquility. Cylinder models, while they might require more strength, are quiet and green substitutes. ⬤

Wellingtons

Invented by the Duke of Wellington, this rubber boot made its way from the battlefield into the high fashion of the mid-nineteenth century, and wound up a faithful companion to today's gardeners the world over. The long shaft of the boot defends against bothersome thorns and branches, and the rubber acts as a waterproofing material that can be easily cleaned. This convenient set of properties allows gardeners to enter deep into their plots and vegetable patches, even in bad weather. ━━●

Room to Grow

The good, the bad, and the ugly: Getting acquainted
to the backyard garden

Digging In

Gardens are products of their environments, and as such are defined by temperature, materials, and means. While it is key to have an initial idea of what you would like your garden to look like, gardening is an activity both ongoing and evanescent, incorporating trial-and-error as much as taste. For those starting out, flowers will lend instant aesthetic appeal, while a raised bed will make everything from planting, harvesting, and weed control easier.

Good to Know: Beginner gardeners looking to grow vegetables should limit themselves to a select few favorites, choosing plants that not only grow well in the local area, but also grow well together. ——•

Taking Decisions Lightly

Where you plant what should not be a random choice, but a decision strongly influenced by the amount of sunlight different areas of your yard garner. Herb or vegetable gardens will need four to six hours of direct sunlight a day, and planting these closer to home can make sense in terms of harvesting. Cacti and succulents will happily be placed at a distance from the watering system, in a dry and sunny location.

Good to Know: Harvesting should take place when produce is at its peak, which means during the early hours before the sun wilts plants' leaves. —•

Liquid Sustenance

Among the many rules of nature that gardeners need to obey, the quantity of water available is one of the most vital. During warmer months, plants should be watered thoroughly in the morning and evening to avoid evaporation or burning the leaves. Consider where the water will drain and the extremities of weather. Sustainable gardeners will make use of collected rainwater, fully utilizing natural resources.

Good to Know: To help the ground retain moisture, an extra layer of mulch on top of the soil is an ideal addition. —•

Spacing Out

For bigger gardens, zoning in on an area of the yard and certain plants lays the ground for green success. So-called "foundation plants" work best around the home garden to adorn it all year round—these include shrubs, small trees, perennials, and annuals. More advanced gardeners might work towards an island bed at the yard's center. Fences and house walls make ideal locations for plant vines. Larger-growing plants can provide privacy around the yard's edges.

Good to Know: In smaller gardens, do not waste space by growing the biggest vegetable varieties. Instead of a beefsteak tomato, try a cherry tomato, which grows more easily and yields more fruit. —•

Where the Wild Things Grow (and Go)

Unwanted plants will steal away vital nutrients, sunlight, and water, but taking out the riff-raff should not necessarily mean throwing them onto the compost pile. Not all weeds should be weeded out—in fact some have their best moments on top of our salads.

At the same time, we should appreciate the creatures that dwell and scuttle through our garden, those that are perhaps the beneficiaries of our labor, but also those that keep the garden in good health. Flowers, including lavender, chamomile, dill, and parsley, attract bees and butterflies while warding off pests. —•

5 Wild Weeds to Savor

1. Dandelion greens
2. Chickweed
3. Lamb's Quarter
4. Pepper Cress
5. Stinging Nettles

I would always recommend that people grow what they eat a lot of, and food that's suitable to their region.

Lisa Giroday, Victory Gardens

Before Buying: Plants & Pots, Tips by Lisa Giroday

1. Always buy organic, including soil, seeds, vegetables, and herb starts
2. Know your region
3. Grow what you spend most on in the grocery store
4. Be conscious of the size of your pots in relation to what you want to grow
5. Don't be shy! Experiments in the garden can be the best learning opportunities!

Shades of Green

If it grows together, it goes together. Indeed, mixing herb and vegetable gardens benefits the growth of your plants. A common combination is basil grown beside tomatoes, which helps rid the tomato leaves of the bugs that chew on them. Other magical combinations include beans and potatoes, lettuces with other greens such as spinach or kale, as well as mint and chives with eggplant.

Good to Know: Mix plants of similar sizes, shapes, and ripening times for a more efficient use of space and to avoid shading smaller plants. ──●

Ready, Set, Sow

The basis of growing from seed is healthy soil, which should be crumbly when dug up—growing grasses are an indicator that the earth is in good shape. Newly planted seeds should not feel overcrowded, and need extra attention with plenty of water and a shield from hard sunlight. An easy way to start growing a garden from seed (es-pecially in colder climates or to jump start your garden during colder months) is to be-gin indoors, where seeds can easily be pro-vided with plenty of light and monitoring. When the seeds germinate, separate them into individual pots. The seeds can be trans-planted once they have developed and the frost date has passed. ⟶●

Plants that Tolerate Being Transplanted

1. Broccoli
2. Brussel sprouts
3. Parsley
4. Leeks
5. Celery

Hilgard Garden: From Concrete Jungle to Zen Escape

Mary Barensfeld
Architecture

Berkeley,
CA, United States

●—— Designed as an extended living space, this modernist garden room is tucked between its neighbors' backyards. The site's eye-catching steep slope is set up as a meandering path adorned with sculptural Japanese maple trees that lead to an upper seating area. An area for entertaining at the garden's base is level with the living room, intended as a seamless continuation of the indoor lounging area. Night lighting, too, makes quite the impact. Backlit triangular LED lights installed on the steps draw the eye to the higher seating area, which boasts views across San Francisco's East Bay. The incorporation of concrete into the design of the garden is a nod to the Bay Area's modern edge, coupled with sustainable building practices, such as greywater drainage and an irrigation system. ——➤

◗━ Conceptualized as an inhabitable piece of furniture, this sheltered retreat provides a space for momentary respite from the everyday. Connected to a private family residence in Bangalore, the pavilion bridges the natural habitats of garden and home. The pavilion was designed with a separate entrance from the street; illuminated by subtle lamps at night, the excavated, sunken path not only provides a shift in acoustics, but also privacy by way of its richly planted surroundings. The architects designed a low bridge made from strips of reclaimed wood, matching the eco-lodge vibe, while physically separating the structure from the home and neighboring city. Acting as a portal, the pavilion stands between two contrasting spaces: a wild, overgrown garden and a calm, habitable seating area. The architects behind CollectiveProject pride themselves on involving the entire architectural landscape to create spatial narratives, rather than

The Garden Pavilion as Exotic Escape

CollectiveProject   Bangalore, India

limiting their creative ability to a project's interior space. For special occasions, the seating area can be cleared to give way to a small stage that the family uses for get-togethers and performances. ➞

143

Winterbourne House & Garden: An Edwardian Gem

Haarkon Plants　　Birmingham, United Kingdom

━━ It was by accident that the plant lovers behind Haarkon stumbled into the Winterbourne Garden, a "secret world in the center of Birmingham with so many visual treats." Home to over 6,000 plant species, the botanic garden covers seven acres and includes the magnificently restored Edwardian Winterbourne House, a woodland walk, and a 1930s Japanese bridge. Plants growing here are native to various corners of the world, from China and South America to alpine regions. As part of the nearby University of Birmingham, Winterbourne Garden offers workshops and seminars for visitors, such as beekeeping, vegetable growing, and hanging basket making. ━━➤

Follow the Signs:
Cactus Gatherings

Haarkon Plants 🌱 North Yorkshire, United Kingdom

●—— India and Magnus of Haarkon Plants inquisitively followed a sign perched atop a garden gate in the village of Robin Hood's Bay, North Yorkshire, and were soon invited to tour a stunning private collection of cacti. Richard, the owner, told the two plant enthusiasts that he had started with one plant for each of his five children, his collection growing from there. A second sign inside the greenhouse emphasizes the heartfelt nature of his collection. It reads, "All money raised by the sale of these plants goes to help children in the Third World." Richard's greenhouse can be found by following the B1447 toward the seaside town of Whitby, keeping an eye out for the signs. ——●

The Root of Things

Digging gems out of empty lots in Vancouver

During the First and Second World Wars, millions of gardens were planted across Canada, Britain, and the United States in an effort to up public food supplies. Governments encouraged these so-called war gardens or victory gardens to help citizens reduce consumption and grow their own produce. In taking over residential backyards and public spaces, from church grounds to city parks, digging for a greener future came with a simpler lifestyle that helped avoid rationing.

Fast forward to Vancouver 2012, where long-time friends Lisa Giroday, Sam Philips, and Sandra Lopuch launched Victory Gardens. Looking back to move forward, the homegrown enterprise builds on war gardening's root principles. The group's first conversation on the project began organically in Lisa's garden. "As friends, environmentalists, gardeners, and advocates of and for sustainable food, we wanted to stay in the city, grow food, and encourage people to rethink how they used their spaces," Giroday says.

Contrary to farming during wartime, sustainable living has taken a front seat not only in rural environments but urban ones, too. Here especially, where the air is dense and the availability of space slim, people seek a natural escape. Longevity, coupled with readily available information on the positive impact of a nutrient-rich diet, has inspired consumers to go back to humble agrarian roots. "From what we have learned about how destructive industrial farming is and how pervasive food waste is, there's no disregarding the trend towards sustainable food systems. We can say with certainty that every one of our customers understands why it's important to consume organically, locally, and sustainably," Sam says.

Victory Gardens' revamped model offers everything from developing and designing infrastructure to educating people on growing organic produce, or helping to produce food for those who do not have the time, space, or skills to do so. Additionally, the team hosts workshops based on 365 days of growing, covering topics such as soil preparation, seeding, and transplanting

As friends, environmentalists, gardeners, and advocates of and for sustainable food, we wanted to stay in the city, grow food, and encourage people to rethink how they used their spaces.

Lisa Giroday

starter plants. Although it is not likely that all of Victory Gardens' customers will become farmers, any amount they can grow has an incredibly positive impact.

Each of the co-founders brings a unique skillset to the table, with backgrounds in environmental studies, industrial design, and master gardening between them. As a result of changes to her own health and wellness practices, Lisa's full-time interest in gardening began with unpacking the meaning behind eating good food. Starting with a small raised bed, she dug her way to a full front and backyard with self-taught competence. "We tend to speak very affectionately about the importance of connecting to the earth, and, when given the opportunity to work the soil, we see what can be grown in small amounts of space while experiencing catharsis through these growing activities," she says.

The group's interest also lies in the effect gardening has on mental wellness by promoting physical activity and healthy eating habits—a gateway drug to sustainable consumption. The fostering of community ties, too, has the power to bring about meaningful change. Bringing people back together to learn the lost art of basic food production is a mission the young team has elevated from an idea to a thriving, sustainable startup. They promote important work that looks good, functions perfectly, and pays off. ➝

Framing Growth in a Multicultural Community

Lucas Foglia  Providence, RI, United States

◆—— In Providence, Rhode Island, photographer Lucas Foglia documented urban farming communities at the Somerset Community Garden for two years. Here, the garden's 72 plots are tended by families from African-American, European, Cambodian, Dominican, Hmong, Laotian, and Liberian backgrounds. Members come together for the practical purpose of providing for their families, but also to learn about gardening, composting, and preserving in environmentally sustainable ways. In turn, coming together has fostered a cross-cultural dialog where people share tools, skills, and stories. Foglia's photography benefits from his involvement in the cultural fabric of the place, the resulting images from his two-year project becoming a window into the lives of a small, thriving community. ——◆

On Homegrown Wellness
with Grown & Gathered

Grown & Gathered /
Lentil and Matt Purbrick

Tabilk, Victoria,
Australia

●—— Outside of Melbourne, a small organic farm is making waves among locals and top chefs alike. Run by Lentil and Matt Purbrick, Grown & Gathered is a business very much based on traditional, pre-industrial practices and ways of living. Their vegetables, fruits, and flowers are seasonally harvested from their three-acre waste-free farm, located in the town of Tabilk, Victoria. While extending their philosophy of nourished living to the hunting and gathering of wild foods, Lentil and Matt nurture animals and pickle and preserve from home. Living with plants came naturally for the duo, who left their careers in the city for a simpler life in tune with nature. With a reverence for wholesome, organic food, they successfully branched out and began selling their produce to Melbourne's top chefs, restaurants, and cafés. Lentil and Matt are now digging deeper, running workshops and talks, and educating locals, businesses, and farms on everything from age-old sustainability skills to waste-free living, preservation, and food preparation. Whether living in a city, town, or in the countryside, the pair know that working alongside nature and providing favorable conditions for produce to grow will open up a whole new world of homegrown wellness. ——●

One Cactus Store To Rule Them All

Carlos Morera,
John Morera

Los Angeles,
CA, United States

In a tiny storefront in Los Angeles' Echo Park, Carlos Morera and his uncle John cram cacti of all shapes and sizes–rare, bizarre, and beautiful to behold. Cactus Store is a humble neighborhood space that showcases this unusual collection of John Morera's, a longtime bonsai guru and veteran nurseryman. Plants range in price from $20 to $2,000, and are displayed and sold in terracotta pots that sit on stacked cinder blocks. Never will you see a delivery truck pull up with 30 of the same cactus. The duo travel across the country looking for unique specimens to bring back to their shop, buying plants from farms and collectors to uphold the variety on offer. Being related does not always mean sharing the same taste, and Carlos and John Morera find it interesting how each person coming into the store connects with a different plant. "Perhaps you can just sense a connection subconsciously," Carlos says.

162

Cactus Country, As Far as the Eye Can See

Jim Hall, Photography by Emma Perry   Strathmerton, Australia

●—— In a small country town in Victoria, Australia, one man's fascination with cacti and succulents has grown far beyond its envisioned proportions. Jim Hall and his wife Julie took over Cactus Country when Hall's father was in search of a suitable bidder for his unique collection in 1979. With no gardening experience up their sleeves, the couple decided to take the leap and approach the garden as a business opportunity. Nonetheless, Cactus Country is a collection grown from love; from the beginning, Jim was fascinated by visitors' reactions to the varied cacti–their odd shapes, and their shades of green, yellow, and pink dotting the landscape. The couple propagated new seeds and planted a variety of larger species over four years, taking on side jobs at local orchards, and growing strawberries and tomatoes to finance their dream of turning the garden into a tourist attraction. In 1984 the couple purchased an additional cactus collection. Today, Cactus Country covers over 40,000-square-meters of land with over 3,000 different plant species. ——➤

Floating Gardens, for the Pond and Tabletop

Seerosenfarm ❧ Rietz-Neuendorf, Germany

●—— A family enterprise with humble ambitions, this water lily farm located in the municipality of Rietz-Neuendorf, between Berlin and the town Frankfurt Oder, enlivens the village during harvest season. Tropical water lilies, lotus flowers, and water plants grow in greenhouses, and can be bought potted or as cut flowers. Every year the family grind, sow, and grow water lotus out of their own harvested seeds. The business is spearheaded by Christian Meyer, who started growing water lilies for commercial purposes in ponds he built in his grandmother's backyard. Seerosenfarm is particularly proud of their homemade lily varieties. ——●

At Stedsans, Home is Where the Harvest is

Flemming Schiøtt Hansen, Mette Helbæk

Copenhagen, Denmark

◂— In Copenhagen, the world's most sustainable eatery is in the making. Until 2014, ØsterGRO was limited to its rooftop farm, a 600-square-meter space divided into vegetable patches, a chicken coop with 12 hens, hives with four families of bees, and compost rich with well-nourished worms. In the summer of 2015 the space expanded its sustainable mission with the greenhouse restaurant Stedsans. Boasting views across the capital's rooftops, Stedsans may be small, but it supplies a mighty few with organically grown produce. Dining here is communal, and the menu changes weekly, offering six farm-fresh dishes served on large sharing plates. Stedsans prides itself in serving food that is minimally altered and always at its prime, "the types of things that taste great without having to mess with them too much," says the owner and chef, Flemming Schiøtt Hansen. —▸

Cultivating Ground in a Post-Urban Future

Hong Kong Value Farm Hong Kong

In Shenzhen, the rooftop of a former glass factory has been transformed into a fertile farm, cultivating communities and sustainable living

It was during the Bi-City Biennale of Urbanism and Architecture in 2013 that Thomas Chung, an associate professor at the Hong Kong School of Architecture, got to thinking about the value of empty rooftops. The former Guangdong Glass Factory that houses the Biennale was once at the center of a thriving industrial zone, a symbol of China's role at the forefront of manufacturing technology.

The abandoned glass factory was transformed into the Value Factory within ten months, and later into Value Farm, with creative director Ole Bouman leading a team of international architects on the project. While Value Factory is a culturally oriented space, offering seminars, workshops, and lectures in conjunction with the Biennale, Value Farm revalorizes the open space on the building's rooftop, providing a permanent regenerative landscape infrastructure. "Early on, the idea of making an urban farm

came from my intention to bring an alternative and unexpected Hong Kong dimension to the Shenzhen site," Chung recalls, "to showcase the emerging Hong Kong, rather than a familiar image of malls and high-rise office towers."

The growing number of rooftop farms popping up around Hong Kong's dense urban landscape provided inspiration for Value Farm. The new ecological environment connects city dwellers to a small-scale hands-on experience in crop-growing. Chung also has big dreams for the demolished market area surrounding Value Farm, as he and the team hope to turn it into productive farming terrain. "For Hong Kong, a hyper-dense vertical metropolis, farming in the city seems counterintuitive. With agricultural terrain occupying 1.6 percent of Hong Kong's land, and providing less than 3 percent of locally produced vegetables, urban farming offers an alternative interaction between the land and people." And the benefits are

sky-high. Chung continues, "It can improve the microclimate of cityscapes while reducing pollution, increase energy-saving food production, contribute to food safety, and provide urban dwellers with the opportunity for physical exercise," to name only a few green benefits.

Covering 2,100-square-meters, Value Farm produces edible plants in an ensemble of plots, platforms, and pavilions. Taking harvesting cycles into account, the team chooses crops based on both their nutritional and aesthetic significance. The crop covering the largest area, for instance, is winter wheat, an agricultural staple in Southern China that recalls ancient agricultural memories. Flaxseed, too, is steeped in history, and is used for various culinary and medicinal purposes. In contrast, the farm features a colorful palette of vegetables, including radicchio, lolla rossa, beetroot, and swiss chard. Local farmers and community enthusiasts maintain the farm through each season, and have begun taking ownership of crop maintenance, organizing activities and building a close-knit farming community.

"Hongkongers are extreme urbanites, and at the beginning we were surprised that young people and students were enthusiastic about participating," Chung says.

"The success of Value Farm has allowed us to pursue other projects. We were able to convince the School of Architecture, where I work, to convert the rooftop lawn into different growing areas, which has turned into the 'Rooftop Cultivation at CUHK' project."

The opportunity for residents in a city like Hong Kong to swap out high-density living for high-density planting is a refreshing one. The recreational and restorative value of urban farming has an increasing importance in today's world, connecting people to nature, fostering local social networks, and educating communities about healthy eating. Without question, the revitalization of this former glass factory into both a public garden and community farm is a shinning model for sustainable initiatives. "The masterplan for the whole of the former glass factory and surrounding areas is being refined, ongoing, and might soon include innovative technology startups in the factory buildings," Chung says. "Nature is being excavated anew from Hong Kong's urban past; rooftop configurations become new ground to cultivate plants in a post-urban future." ➝

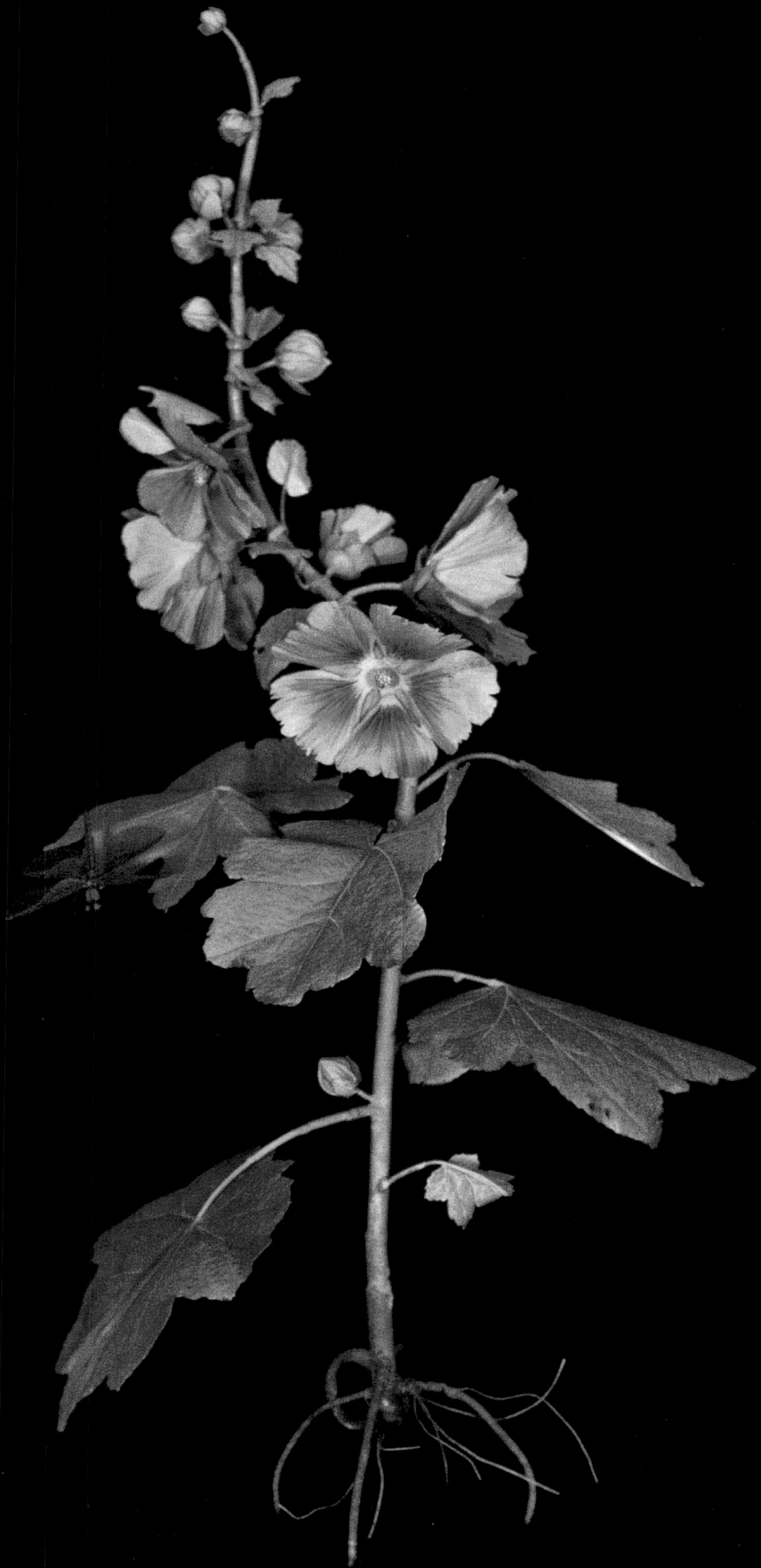

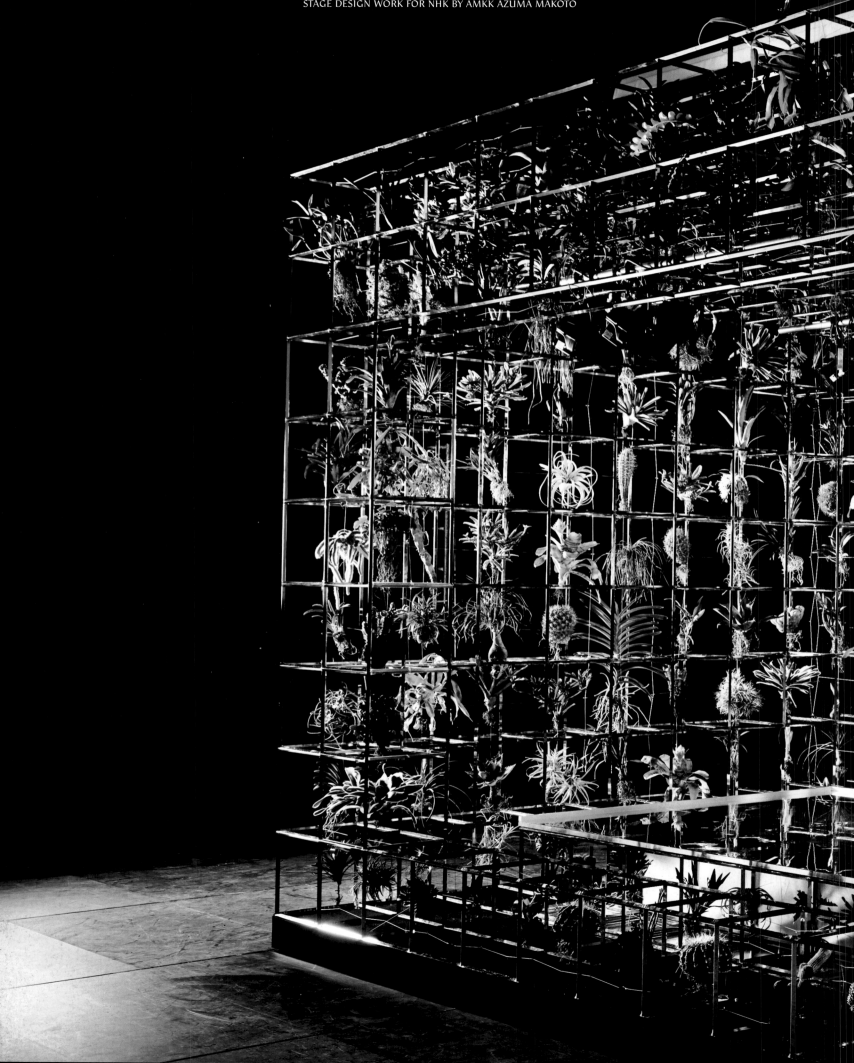

The Continuing Saga of the Garden

Satoshi Kawamoto Tokyo, Japan

Satoshi Kawamoto, a revered Japanese plant stylist, opens the conversation between unruly houseplants and delicate botanicals

In Tokyo, Satoshi Kawamoto has already opened seven of his Green Fingers boutiques, each saturated with dark, leafy vines and a storm of foliage. Here, the artist presents not only plants and botanicals, but also a selection of decorative interior items, art, lighting, and vintage clothing. His most recent store in New York's Lower East Side, Green Fingers Market, may be a little more toned-down than its Tokyo counterparts, but at its core holds the same resourceful approach to nature-inspired interiors.

The energetic creative director oversees ten stores across Japan and the United States, while also working across a variety of other genres, styling the interiors of homes, cafés, and department stores. Kawamoto also runs a wedding brand called FORQUE, where he matches bold floral arrangements to a range of venues. To him, the world of greenery is laced with a sense of familiarity, even though the process of creating a garden is evanescent and incomplete by nature. "A garden is a continuing saga. Just as a garden grows bit by bit, a garden blooms with character with each added touch," Kawamoto says. "This holds true for interiors as well: you paint a piece; the paint chips off; you paint it again. It is the process that gives the depth, something that a new piece will never have."

Bringing his plants' personalities to the fore is something the artist likes to describe as "green expression." Although Kawamoto does not see his style as conforming to a certain category, his work is always instilled with something grungy, wild, and alive with green vitality. At the same time, he admires a flower's process of decay, with dried leaves and petals elevating rather than wearing out the essence of a bouquet. For Kawamoto, less is not more, but rather the opposite. His energized environments and sprawling gardens all have a secretive, intriguing quality to them.

For houseplant novices, the master plant stylist says that understanding plants by way of their healing

Just as a garden grows bit by bit, a garden blooms with character with each added touch.

Satoshi Kawamoto

and regenerative qualities is key to opening up a home, awarding a space the feeling of being lived in. Mindful assembling of houseplants is also key; bunching them in certain layers and on different levels of height can bring about a new sense of space. "To create dimension, start with larger plants in the back, adding smaller plants as you work your way forward," Kawamoto says. "Small crates to place plants on are good tools to optimize space, and always be mindful of other colors in the room when choosing plants." While these loose instructions echo Kawamoto's ordered chaos, they also speak to his philosophy of finding beauty in imperfection; a fusion of colors, textures, and shapes serve as his formula for inspiring new relationships to flora and fauna.

Back in the day, Kawamoto started his home collection with a pencil cactus, an easy-care succulent named after its pencil-thin branches. Today, he cares for a personal collection of 50 types of plants, which he maintains as diligently as every garden he exhibits around the world. Kawamoto cites his "Here And There" exhibition at Tokyo's Laforet Harajuku department store as the most memorable project he has worked on, which presented plants taking over interior spaces. "I grew up in an environment with many plants and taught myself everything I know," says the artist. "I like keeping my future uncertain, just like the incomplete nature of gardening, and the blooming of flowers from season to season." ⟶

Loose Leaf: Welcome to the Jungle's Showroom

Charlie Lawler, Wona Bae  Melbourne, Australia

●——— More of an experience than a retail space, Loose Leaf in the heart of Melbourne invites visitors into a lofty world of vivid greenery. Run by husband and wife duo Charlie Lawler and Wona Bae, the converted warehouse is filled with indoor plants and delicate flowers. The showroom-like space could easily double as a botanical gallery, where installations and products come to life in the company of tropical palms dancing across light-bathed walls. Growing up outside the city, Bae on a flower farm in South Korea and Lawler at his grandparents' plant nursery, the couple are keen to surprise customers with nature's offerings. In the evenings, visitors come for in-store classes, getting their hands dirty with terrarium-building, loose-style bouquet making, and floral table arrangements. The design studio arm of their business specializes in landscape design and botanical installations, driven by their motto of observing and experimenting with nature. ——▶

Fashion's Favorite Florist

Thierry Boutemy  Brussels, Belgium

— Belgian florist Thierry Boutemy is one of the most revered botanical artists in the fashion world, his career having received a kickstart after his work was featured in Sofia Coppola's 2006 film, Marie Antoinette. Boutemy's style captures the feeling of stepping into a scene both wild and wonderful, as he works the floral displays on runways for designers such as Dries Van Noten and Lanvin. Dreamlike woods; rose-covered façades; orchards of fragrant flora; a bountiful harvest–these are the scenes his exhibitions and installations convey. Fashion may have long had a penchant for the naturalistic, but with time nature has grown from being a subsidiary to a bold statement, as shown through Boutemy's intuitive combinations of twigs, branches, and wild flowers. —

The Secret Life of Plants

Stéphane Margolis  Paris, France

━━ Threatening and beautiful at once is how Stéphane Margolis interprets and displays nature. His works in his Toxic Plants series challenge the innocence of flora and fauna, transforming plants and flowers into surrealist forms by adding artificial materials to them. Growing up in the horticultural region of Hyéres in the south of France, Margolis is inspired by memories of blossoming plantations and sprawling landscapes. Coupled with his professional training in the Japanese art of floral arrangement, ikebana, his creations are a reminder of the fragility of our planet. The presentation of his plants demonstrates not only how richly versatile the natural world is, but also the extent to which we must preserve its seductions. ━━

219

Natural Remedies

Antonino Sciortino Milan, Italy

In Milan, the designer Antonino Sciortino dresses his home with plants reminiscent of a childhood in Sicily

Growing up between the ocean and the olive groves of Sicily, the Italian designer Antonino Sciortino's Milan home is filled with memories of his childhood. Originally the industrial building had been an atelier used for the manufacturing of glass covers for electric calculators. Its generous dimensions and outdoor garden ticked all the boxes for the sculptor, who was looking for a comfortable space in which to both live and work.

Sciortino was born in 1962 in Bagheria, a quaint seaside town located in the province of Palermo. At the age of eight, he found a love for working with metal in his father's workshop, where he spent countless hours bending wires to form small lamps and objects. At 16, Sciortino discovered his dancing feet, secretly escaping

the workshop to take evening courses in Palermo. He then moved to Rome, working in dance and choreography for television and theater for nearly 20 years, before settling into his Milan home.

The 200-square-meter loft is located on Via Savona in Milan's Zona Tortona neighborhood, which is known for its thriving contemporary art scene. Extending across two levels, the Italian maker's home is surprisingly silent at the city's center, and benefits from floor-to-ceiling windows that flood the space with light. Around the back of the loft, garden views abound–a rarity and privilege in Milan. The designer successfully evoked the feeling of living in the countryside by creating harmony between the outdoor vegetation and his impressive collection of indoor plants. Palm trees, olive trees, bamboo,

cacti, and succulents stand in sturdy planters and terra-cotta pots, each handpicked with Sciortino's innate eye for design. Every corner of the home has been carefully assembled, creating an atmosphere that balances the intimately nostalgic with the daringly modern.

As an artist, Sciortino specializes in crafted interior objects and furnishings. He patiently renovated the home to include a workshop, where his metal sculptures, tables, vases, and artworks are molded, shaped, and brought to life. The minimalist sculptures, vegetation, and isolated elements of graphic color play off the rawness of the interior and add a warm character to the retreat. When entertaining buyers, Sciortino can also use the ground floor as a showroom to present the work within a natural context.

Sciortino describes his own style as minimalist baroque. Indeed, wooden accents mingle with the loft's concrete and steel. "I never followed fashion or anything that works in a specific moment," says Sciortino.

"If my house is considered trendy I think that's because it's so strongly personal and natural, instinctive. A home should be furnished for ourselves, and no others."

Influences from growing up among the elements of earth and sea can be felt everywhere in the loft. Sicily is alive in many shapes and forms. A red lacquer dining table made of lava stone from Mount Etna was bought in a village near the volcano. The courtyard reflects the silver shine of olive trees. The bathroom is the only room where bright colors lead: a wall of turquoise tiles borrows from the deep blue of the Mediterranean Sea. Plants, like many other things in the artist's home, have a personal quality to them, comforting and awakening at once. "Every object I have comes from my travels and represents an emotion that I met in my life. All plants in my house are Sicilian. I like things that are able to communicate emotions, things that have a certain substance, independent of whether they are old or new." ⟶

Escape to the City:
A Weekend Home in São Paulo

SPBR Arquitetos, Angelo Bucci 🌱 São Paulo, Brazil

⬤—— Centrally located in the metropolis of São Paulo, this home transforms life in a city of 20 million people into a holiday destination. While countless residents flee the urban heat on the weekends to escape to the coast, this home was designed to save the time spent commuting in favor of a downtown destination. Stacked across three floors, the house comes together in an interesting interplay of vertical volumes. The home's central elements are the garden, swimming pool, and solarium, with the ground level kept relatively free of construction to maximize garden space. The standout feature, though, is surely the "floating" swimming pool. Visible from the street, it rests six meters above ground level in a volume of exposed concrete. ——➤

The Many Faces of Casa Goia

Renata Pati   São Paulo, Brazil

In São Paulo, this dreamy green home might look like the ideal summer rental, but is actually an events venue and hotspot for creative gatherings. When the house that stood in its place was torn down, architect Renata Pati reincorporated elements such as the brick structure and wooden beams, using them as flooring and a pergola. Inside, Casa Goia is multifunctional and constantly evolving; one night the venue plays host to a lively product launch and the next it becomes an art gallery or co-working space. The multifarious nature of Casa Goia is emphasized by its open design, the floors flooded with natural light and enriched with greenery. Out back, vertical gardens of native plants and decked walls surround the swimming pool. Together with sturdy, earthy elements, such as cracked concrete, rusty iron, and wood, the homey space gives way to something naturally imperfect. ⟶

Camouflage Cabins in Mill Valley, California

Feldman Architecture  Mill Valley, CA, United States

━ Nestled on an overgrown slope north of San Francisco, this multifunctional home, built for an artist and gardener, was designed based on a brief asking for both a yoga studio and an art studio. Its location within the woods offers privacy and seclusion in the company of towering pine trees and redwoods. The site itself was only minimally regraded, while the planted roof of the lower-sitting yoga studio is covered in a carpet of succulents, offering an inspiring view from the artist's studio above. Seemingly camouflaged into the surrounding environment, the cabin housing the art studio boasts clerestory windows and skylights to maximize sunlight. ━

240

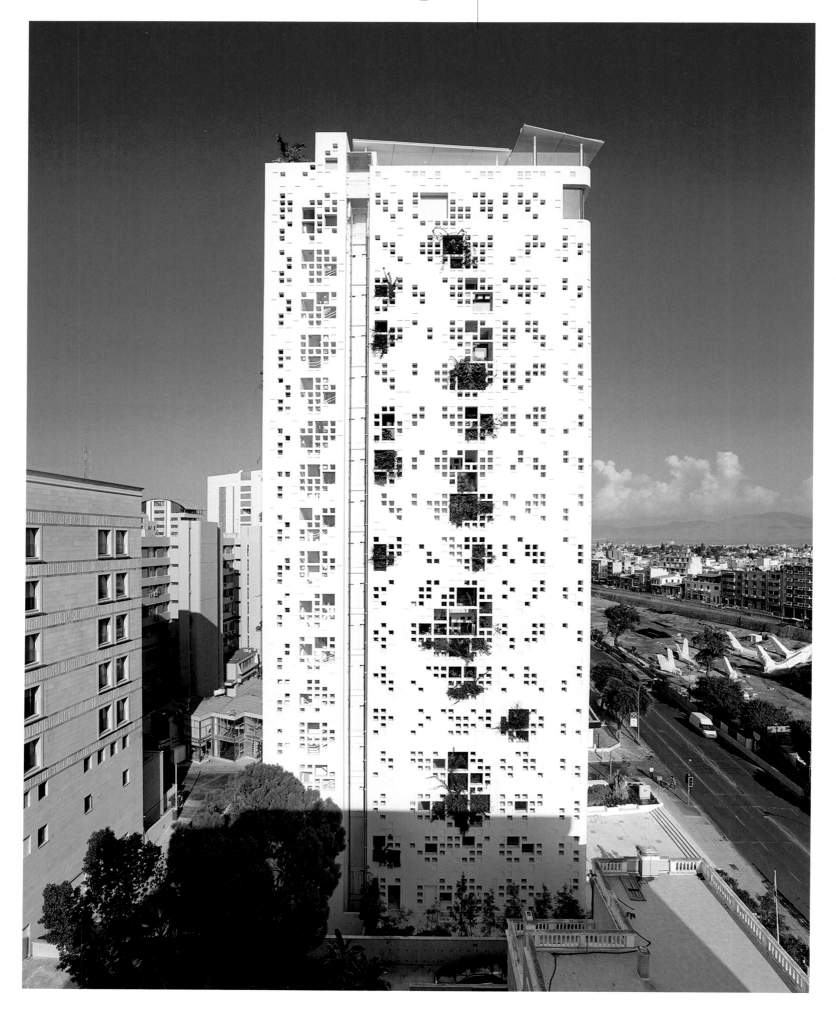

Index

Evergreen

Living with Plants

This book was conceived, edited,
and designed by Gestalten.

Edited by Sven Ehmann, Robert Klanten, and Victoria Pease
Text by Victoria Pease
Additional text by Benjamin Barlow

Editorial management by Maria-Elisabeth Niebius
Copy-editing by Rachel Sampson
Proofreading by Benjamin Barlow

Design and layout by Jonas Herfurth
Creative direction design and cover by Ludwig Wendt
Illustrations by Florian Bayer
Typefaces: Octavius by Hugues Gentile (Foundry: www.gestaltenfonts.com),
Superla Book by Karl-Heinz Lange and Ole Schäfer
Cover image photography by Lorenzo Pennati; styling by
Christina Nava and *Marie Claire Maison Italy*

Printed by Nino Druck GmbH, Neustadt / Weinstraße
Made in Germany

Published by Gestalten, Berlin 2016
ISBN 978-3-89955-673-5

For more information, please visit www.gestalten.com.
Bibliographic information published by the Deutsche Nationalbibliothek.
The Deutsche Nationalbibliothek lists this publication in the
Deutsche Nationalbibliografie; detailed bibliographic data are
available online at http://dnb.d-nb.de.

None of the content in this book was published in exchange for payment by
commercial parties or designers; Gestalten selected all included work based
solely on its artistic merit.

This book was printed on paper certified according to the standard of the FSC®.